BIG
TEAMS

THE KEY INGREDIENTS FOR SUCCESSFULLY DELIVERING LARGE PROJECTS

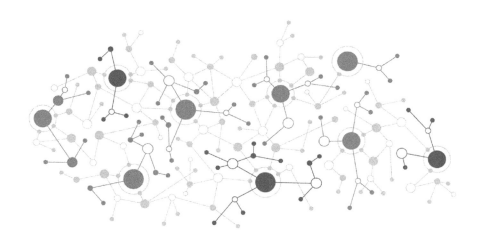

TONY LLEWELLYN

First published in Great Britain by Practical Inspiration Publishing, 2020

© Tony Llewellyn, 2020

The moral rights of the author have been asserted

ISBN   978–1–78860–104–7 (print)
           978–1–78860–127–6 (epub)
           978–1–78860–105–4 (mobi)

Practical Inspiration
PUBLISHING

MIX
Paper from
responsible sources
FSC
www.fsc.org   FSC® C013604

For Ed Moore, who opened the doors that made this book possible

Contents

Figures

Tables

Preface

In the modern workplace, individuals rarely work in isolation but are grouped with other colleagues into notional teams. The degree to which these collections of individuals come together to work as an effective unit is a topic that is of significant interest both to organizations and to academics. Given the right conditions, people working in teams can often achieve amazing outcomes. They can just as easily devolve into dysfunctional groups.

There has consequently been a great deal of research in recent years into the question of how to build an effective team. The attention of most of the research into team performance has tended to consider individual units of between 8 and 12 people. Less attention has been paid to what happens when there is a need to create a very large team of hundreds or even thousands of human beings, all focused on achieving the same outcome. This book takes a step into a void in the literature to consider the challenges and opportunities that arise when creating what might be called a *Big Team*. As will be explained in Chapter 1, Big Teams tend to be found in the world of projects rather than what is often called the business-as-usual operations of a large organization.

The content of this book is structured around a model derived from my research over the past seven years, both as a practising consultant and a part-time academic. I have spent much of my career working in the construction industry where the word 'team' is often used to describe anyone involved at a particular moment in the development of a physical asset. As I shifted my career to become more focused on how to help teams work together more productively, it became clear to me that the people and the organizations involved in the construction process habitually operated in a way that was often dysfunctional. The desire to improve how such large project teams work has been one of the drivers for my continued interest in this field.

As I have expanded my research beyond the construction sector into major projects in other industries, it has been fascinating to see the consistency of the behaviours of humans working in large groups. I have found that irrespective of sector or specialization, people working in large complex projects demonstrate the same propensity for collaborative creativity on the one hand and disruptive conflict on the other. Through the following nine chapters, I will introduce you to the components that have been found to help improve the chances of success, by tapping into the human instinct to work in teams. The content will also help you understand the darker side of human nature, and how the impact of our disruptive tendencies can be diminished.

The book is written in a style that is intended to be informal, but informative. It is not therefore an academic book, but is nevertheless intended to be academically credible. I have tapped into the knowledge and wisdom of numerous authors and have tried to ensure they are credited where appropriate. It has been written for anyone who aspires to take on a leadership role in a major project. The concepts, observations and ideas are also likely to be of interest to a growing segment of professionals who wish to develop their skills as team coaches. I use the term *project leader* and *project manager* as the primary title, but the qualifying attribute is leadership in whatever form or whatever element of a role you may occupy.

My hope is that the content intrigues and inspires you to learn and develop a skill set that I believe will be critical to the world's ability to find answers to the growing need for sustainable infrastructure and technological change. As projects grow in size and complexity, the world needs people who are able to lead and manage the large collections of specialist teams working at scale. This is not easy, as the skills and abilities learned on smaller projects do not automatically transfer to much bigger enterprises. This book is intended to stretch your thinking, and open your mind to a set of alternative possibilities.

The intention is to create some momentum for those engaged in large projects to continue to learn and explore. This book is not a comprehensive compendium of everything you might need to know about leading a Big Team. The content examines a range of specific elements set within a framework for improving team performance. As you will find, there are many additional future paths for a student of human behaviour to explore, but my intention is to present a number of ideas and concepts within a structure that is easy to absorb, understand and apply.

I have a website www.teamcoachingtoolkit.com where I post tools, techniques and other material that might be of interest to anyone who wishes to master the art of shaping team dynamics. You will find I have included links throughout the book to certain pages on the website that provide additional information to support an idea or suggestion made within the framework.

My intention is to continue to study and explore this fascinating area and I am keen to connect with those who share my interest. If you would like to contact me, the best route is through the email address to.llew@mac.com

In the meantime, read on and see where this learning expedition takes you.

Chapter 1
A model of team performance

Big Teams are an essential feature of modern working life. The tasks and challenges faced by people in organizations require the collective skills and knowledge of different people assembled into effective units. Humans have been adept at working cooperatively in groups for thousands of years, but are also equally capable of finding reasons to disagree and disconnect from each other. In the last 50 years or so, leaders and academics have tried to understand the factors that influence a team to achieve results beyond expectations or to fall in to dysfunction. For those interested in teamwork and team development, there is plenty of material to explore. Most of the published research focuses on the dynamics occurring within a small team, usually containing five to ten people. The research also tends to concentrate on static teams working in permanent organizations where a team is regarded as a unit of the organization's structure.

There is relatively little information on another significant segment of the working population world, which operates in the world of projects. Project teams have a different set of internal dynamics, which can both positively and negatively affect how they function. Projects come in many shapes and sizes, some requiring the attention of perhaps a dozen or so people, whilst others may require the skills of thousands. As we move through the change and upheaval of the 21st century, projects are growing in scale, being driven by governments upgrading a country's infrastructure or commercial businesses seeking to take advantage of new opportunities that may have global reach.

Large projects require many people from different professional, technical and social backgrounds to come together and work as a cohesive entity, which can be called a Big Team. The book is written for those who must lead, manage and deliver large projects in which people are assembled in a continually shifting organization structure. The content is therefore focused on how a project or programme is organized and influenced when the number of people involved grows beyond the scale and control of an individual leader. Should you decide to invest some time in learning, you will find there is both an art and a science to the development and maintenance of a Big Team. We will be exploring some of the technical structures and processes that are a part of the organization of a major project but the primary focus is on leadership, and the factors that shape and influence successful Big Teams.

Projects vs business-as-usual

The following chapters are primarily focused on the distinct challenges of working on major projects. The content is less concerned with teams working on day-to-day operations often referred to as business-as-usual. Many enterprises employ large numbers of people to carry out the different functions that the organization needs to deliver its intended purpose. Business-as-usual teams are generally set up as a collection of distinct functions designed to produce specified outputs on a repetitive basis. Over time these functions develop their own distinct subcultures, which tend to limit communication and collaboration with other departments. Whilst the leaders of large permanent organizations might aspire to their staff working as a unified entity, the reality of day-to-day life means that they default to siloed entities, each with their own goals and agendas that rarely translate into a cohesive whole. As we will see, large project teams can also struggle with siloed behaviours, but every new project has the opportunity to establish the right behavioural norms without having to undergo a major transformational change initiative.

It is a frequent observation in the project management literature that projects create *temporary* organizations, which have a number of characteristics that separate them from *permanent* organizations. Ana

Tyssen and her colleagues Andreas Wald and Patrick Speith (2013) set out a number of factors that illustrate this difference:

1. Projects usually have a limited and predefined duration, which compresses the time available to develop the strong cultural norms that are needed to build trust.
2. Large projects invariably have a unique outcome and must rely on creativity and technical knowledge within a set of participants who have only a limited time to get to know each other.
3. Project teams will often have missing hierarchies so that there are gaps or overlaps in authority.
4. Finally, major projects have a high level of uncertainty, creating greater risks, which in turn can reduce commitment when events do not work to plan.

This distinction between permanent and temporary organizations is important. As discussed above, the whole concept of leadership is recognized as a critical success factor to any enterprise that seeks to coordinate the activities of large groups of people. Each of these factors creates distinct challenges for those tasked with leading a project. As complexity within the project environment increases, the limitations imposed by the temporary organizational structure become more critical to the project's performance. Most very large projects are actually made up of a programme of works but, for the sake of brevity, I have used the term *project* to cover both terms.

This does not mean that the contents of this book are irrelevant to business-as-usual teams in permanent organizations. Whilst the challenges of introducing a cohesive culture within a permanent existing organization are quite distinct from those of the project, humans working in groups present the same managerial problems whatever the focus. The concepts and ideas set out in this book therefore apply to many of the situations found in permanent organizations, although obviously the context will differ.

There are a number of core themes that inform the observations, ideas and suggestions contained in the subsequent chapters:

1. a Big Team as a team of teams;
2. the three primary elements of a project;
3. the impact of complexity and uncertainty on major projects; and
4. the behaviours of humans working in groups.

I will now look at each of these in turn.

A Big Team as a team of teams

Before we continue, it is worth exploring what I mean by a 'Big Team'. It is not easy to find a definition of what constitutes a 'big' or a 'large' team. The word *team* tends to be used in the world of projects to include every person engaged on that project and often crosses organizational boundaries. In this context, it is simply a noun used to delineate anyone who may have an active interest in the undertaking. It is often intended to show a degree of inclusivity but the reality is that, as the numbers of people engaged in a project increase, there is not a single big project team, but rather a collection of *small* teams.

There is an important distinction to be made between big and small teams. These simple words explain a much deeper concept. Terms such as small and big are part of our basic language. They can therefore be seen to be generic, having such a wide range of application. In the context of teams, however, these two words have a precise technical role that helps establish some key differences. To emphasize the distinct nature of a Big Team, I will continue to capitalize the term throughout the book.

The small team is the unit of production within any large enterprise. Emperors and generals have historically organized their armies and administrators into manageable groups. This is not, however, a top-down management strategy to create neatly arranged grouping on an 'org chart'. It is actually a reflection of how humans prefer to work with each other. Groups of people naturally fall into sub-groups as the numbers involved start to increase. This is partly because we can typically engage on a regular basis with up to ten people, but beyond that number, communication starts to become more sporadic and building close working relationships is more difficult. In terms of size, Michael West (2012) confirms a commonly held view that effective teams contain fewer than 15 people, and ideally 6–8. It is not possible to define at what point a 'normal' team becomes a Big Team, as the distinction will be specific to the context of the situation. However, as projects scale up in terms of scope, budget and programme length, more people become involved, and will quickly reorganize themselves organize into sub-teams that might be based around function, specialization or just personal preference.

Large projects evolve over time. They typically begin with a core group that takes the project through its preliminary stages, but then the numbers expand rapidly when the programme moves into detailed planning, design and delivery. Some teams come from one organization but major projects also usually draw in many small specialist teams. Some of these small teams are collections of individuals who have worked together before, but others will be newly formed. Whilst every major project has a distinct culture, which affects how it works, each small team will develop its own subculture. This is driven by the team's leaders, by the circumstances of the project and by the other social or commercial elements that tie them together.

The point is that Big Teams do not exist as a single homogeneous whole, shaped by a unitary corporate culture. Instead, a Big Team is an organic collection of individuals and small groups whose roles and activities shift and change as the project they are engaged on progresses. Project success therefore depends upon the extent to which the leadership can enable this assembly of small teams to work effectively together as sub-units that make up a single Big Team.

The danger in writing about projects as a generic term is that the text can lose the nuances and practical observations that are specific to an industry sector, or particular type of project. When exploring the challenges of a software team, the technical processes used will typically be different to those used on an engineering project. When it comes to understanding the behaviours within project teams, however, the primary challenges are very similar. Humans are wired to operate using patterns of behaviour that are, to a certain extent, quite predictable depending upon various factors that shape how they operate as a group.

The three primary elements of a project

Having spent much of the last seven years studying team working on large projects, I have found there are three primary elements to every project, each requiring a distinct area of competence:

- Technical competence – the knowledge and awareness of how components of the project are to be designed and assembled.
- Commercial competence – the knowledge and awareness of issues around money, contracts and the identification and management of risk.
- Social competence – the knowledge and awareness of how humans behave in groups and teams.

Technical competence comes from the years of investment in education and training in a particular profession that an individual chooses as the basis for their future career. This knowledge stays with us as we move from project to project, building as we add new experiences that improve our practical application. Large project teams typically comprise a wide range of specialist professionals each providing a distinct contribution to the design and delivery of the project. Not surprisingly, this is where much of the focus on team selection takes place.

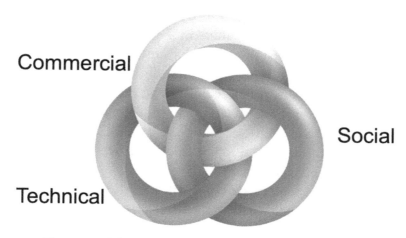

Commercial

Social

Technical

Figure 1.1 The three elements of project competence

Technical skills alone are not sufficient as someone must take care of the money. Whether the project is sponsored by a public or private body, the team must pay attention to *commercial* matters. Budgets must be created and costs monitored. The risks to the project must be identified and mitigated, and processes must be put in place to ensure the governance of the project follows best practice. Project sponsors usually apply considerable resources in the form of lawyers and accountants to ensure that sufficient commercial intelligence is in place.

The third, but least articulated, element is *social* competence. This capability is critical to the manner in which team members interact and work together. Large projects involve lots of people with their individual and idiosyncratic ways. So whilst managers may often wish that people would behave with the predictability of mechanoids, the reality is that skills and knowledge must also be applied to leading, influencing and connecting the diverse members of the wider team to behave as an integrated unit. This social aspect of project design and delivery is often the key ingredient separating project success from failure.

It might appear to be a statement of the blindingly obvious but the reality is that traditional project management practice focuses primarily on the technical and commercial aspects of project delivery, leaving the social element largely to chance. As we will see, this is a dangerous strategy. The illustration in Figure 1.1 shows the three competences as interlinked rings, which cannot be separated. They are irrevocably intertwined. As a team leader, you cannot focus on one at the expense of the others. All three must be worked on to establish the balance required to ensure a satisfactory outcome. Much of this book therefore is concerned with correcting the balance, and encouraging you to develop your own social competence, and then build the process and practice into the wider team.

These three competencies are present in each of us, but rarely in equal proportions. Some professions, particularly engineers, will have a strong focus towards technical intelligence, and will often show limited interest in the commercial and social aspects of a project. Lawyers and commercial managers will, as their role requires, be more focused on the commercial opportunities and constraints. The question that you must ask yourself as a team leader is 'who within our project team is going to maintain the balance by ensuring the critical elements of social intelligence are in place?'

The impact of complexity and uncertainty on major projects

A factor common to any discussion on the nature of modern projects is the need to deal with complexity, uncertainty and ambiguity. Uncertainty is an inevitable feature of project life, in that all major projects start with a large number of decisions yet to be made, and questions to be answered. In the modern world, however, uncertainty also manifests itself in the continual shift of external influences as wider political, social and technical factors create tensions that disrupt a team's ability to accurately anticipate future events. Human beings dislike uncertainty, particularly in situations that feel threatening, and where possible will try to find ways to manage unknown factors.

David Cleden (2009) points out that managing uncertainty is not the same as managing risk, in that risks can usually be conceived as a threat, quantified in terms of likelihood and severity of consequences, and actions taken to mitigate. Uncertainty is much more difficult to analyse. It is intangible in so far as we simply do not know what is likely to happen until a problem manifests itself. Trying to map out uncertainty within a major project can become a hypothetical exercise that will produce limited practical reward. A more practical place to focus on is the uncertainty that arises because we do not have the knowledge or information to predict exactly what will happen.

In the context of a project, complexity can be understood as a situation in which there are many interconnected variables such as time, scope, budget, resources, stakeholder needs, etc. Each variable exerts pressure on the others in a ways that are not immediately obvious. It can be difficult to match this theoretical description with the potential reality of a project. At what stage does a project shift from being merely complicated to being complex? I have found many senior managers begin a project with a simplistic view of the challenges ahead, and have difficulty recognizing when multiple coinciding issues are likely to create significant problems downstream. I have therefore found it useful to think about complexity in terms of the overlapping influence of the technical, commercial and social elements discussed above.

Technical complexity – Most major projects are likely to involve some degree of technical innovation, often driven by a need for efficiency. The problem with innovation is that it requires experimentation, and the patience to work through a number of iterations before settling on the best solution. Complexity increases when multiple new technologies are being used, which must then learn to interface with each other.

Commercial complexity – Complex projects often start without a firm design, where it is not possible (or at least not sensible) to enter into the type of fixed-price arrangement normally associated with traditional contracts. Fluidity of design, whilst working to tight deadlines, requires a different type of relationship between the parties involved. Simple projects where the design outcome is familiar to all parties can succeed using basic transactional mechanisms. Complexity requires a different approach, where the parties must develop the project scheme together, each adding their specialist knowledge as pieces that come together to solve the puzzle.

Social complexity – As we will discuss in later chapters, human beings frequently have periods when their decision making is based on emotional influence rather than rational thought. Major projects fundamentally rely on people to deliver the thousands of tasks that are needed to achieve the desired output, working in small teams that must connect, communicate and collaborate with each other. Whilst behaviours can be influenced, the actual behaviour of any human on a particular day cannot be accurately predicted, adding a degree of uncertainty into any planning exercise.

As discussed above, the issues that arise from these three elements are continually interconnected and will have an influence on virtually every problem encountered as a major project moves through its cycle. The theme of acknowledging and accommodating complexity and uncertainty therefore informs many of the ideas set out in the following chapters.

The behaviours of humans working in groups

The fourth key theme that runs throughout the book is the behavioural dynamics of humans working in groups. The ability of humans to cooperate with each other is hard wired into our genetic framework. This does not, however, mean that we are naturally good at teamwork as we also have an innate tendency to compete with each other. You do not need to be an expert in behavioural science to recognize that people are not automatically programmed to communicate effectively with others they do not know. Simply assembling a large group of people and expecting them to work as a collective unit is unlikely to produce an instantly organized and focused team.

When faced with a big enough problem however, people can find a way to work together in large numbers. When committed to a common cause, large groups can achieve quite astonishing results. The challenge, then, is to understand the factors that influence the dynamics of teams, and how to encourage the positive elements that will help build trust and collaboration, whilst avoiding the issues that accelerate disengagement and dysfunction.

Case stories

For the past seven years I have been researching the topic of project teams and have taken as many opportunities as I could to interview experienced project leaders and to record their stories. Stories from case studies differ in that they tend to rely on unreliable memories and are inevitably prone to distortion and exaggeration. They are, however, the most powerful way of making a point that will be remembered. Whilst we have known for thousands of years that stories are a highly effective mechanism for passing on information, through advances in neuroscience we now know that we store our memories of stories in a different part of the brain. When we listen to a story, the parts of our brains that deal with language processing become activated to decode the meaning. This happens when we start to take in any form of new information, but when we hear a story our emotions also become aroused, stimulating a wider potential range of response. Feel-good chemicals such as serotonin, dopamine and oxytocin are produced as we react to thoughts that resonate with our own experiences.

Throughout the book I have used many of these stories to illustrate the themes I wish to explore. Many of the stories come from the world of infrastructure and construction, since this is the industry that currently takes up much of my time. I have, however, also found stories of Big Teams delivering mining, engineering and technology projects and programmes. When reading through my notes on each of the stories, it is interesting how little variation is created in a particular sector. There are inevitably distinct technical challenges between the creations of a new mine and delivering a major technology project. People, however, for all our individual quirks and foibles, are a constant in that our work behaviours are largely shaped by the environment we work in and the teams that we are a part of. Peter's story which is described on the next page could apply to any major project.

PETER'S STORY

A couple of years ago I was leading a small group that was part of a large team working on a major engineering project. We had won the bid largely based on our reputation for managing the technical challenges of similar projects. This new project was, however, a big step up in size and scope. It was also politically sensitive. The team had to mobilize quickly and grew from 10 people in the first month to over 140 by month three. About a third of the people came from within our firm. The rest were all in teams of specialist contractors. The timescales for the project were very tight and so little time was set aside for planning. We were enthusiastic about the challenge and just wanted to get on with it, so no time was spent in thinking about how we would work together as an effective team. We structured the sub-groups around our different functional specializations such as design, engineering, commercial, safety and administration. Consequently, rather than a working as a single unit, we were actually just a set of loosely connected teams, effectively, a number of 'silos'. Within my team I found that each person's day-to-day routines involved connections with others in their specialist area, but we had very limited contact with others outside of our own function. We all became very internally focused and interaction was limited to formal meetings, with very little informal communication. The programme started to slip as pressure started to build around the first major deadline.

Our response was to blame the other teams for delays and incomplete work. I could see that relationships between the team leaders became strained as each team focused on their perceived part of the programme. Senior leadership team meetings became formal, with very little social engagement. The project director was a talented engineer with a track record of delivering a number of difficult projects. He was an introverted thinker who liked to take his time to work through issues and was more comfortable with technical solutions than managing personal relationships. I think he was poorly equipped to deal with the tensions building within his team and avoided intervening, even when open squabbles broke out between the team leaders.

Within six months the project team had become so internally focused that communication with the client and the other project stakeholders became strained. I noticed that the stakeholders appeared to be losing confidence in our ability to deliver the project, and we started to get more pressure from them to provide additional information to relieve their concerns. When we failed to achieve the first critical milestone required for the project to proceed, our managing director was called into a meeting with the sponsors and given feedback that our team was not delivering to expectations. He was told that the project would be cancelled unless we could demonstrate a more effective approach.

In some ways, this was the best thing that could have happened. All of the team leaders agreed that we needed to find a better way of working, and so we did a 'reset' and started again from scratch. We spent two days off-site looking openly and honestly at what had happened and what we needed to do to improve. It was all about behaviours, how we communicated and how we needed to build trust within the different sub-teams. We agreed a plan and then kept revisiting it over the next few months to check we were still working to the agreed behaviours.

The outcome was that we got the project back on track. I left the project a year later when our part of the programme was complete, but I hear that it is still going well despite all of the usual difficulties that come with very big projects. It was a great learning experience and I have been able to take a lot of the lessons learned into my next project.

I have come across the themes in this story many times over the past few years as I have collected stories of project success and project failure. The project director and his colleagues who led this project did nothing technically wrong, as they simply followed the process and procedures that had worked quite adequately on smaller projects. The mistake the leadership made was to assume that the people engaged on this bigger project would naturally work together as a cohesive group. This is a bold assumption for a team of any size but, as we shall see, as the groups of people engaged in a shared endeavour grow, the complexities of human relationships become more difficult to monitor and to manage. As my research has shown, the bigger the team, the more attention must be paid to the mechanisms required to encourage the people to work as a collective, rather than competing sub-groups.

Effective teams

When working with project leaders, I frequently hear the desire to create a high-performing team, without having a clear idea as to what high performance actually entails. For some project managers, the requirement is that every member of the team exerts themselves to the limits of their endurance. For others, it just means the team works well together and meets the sponsors' desired outcomes. What constitutes performance is therefore subjective, depending upon the expectations of a particular team. When working with a collection of teams that make up a Big Team however, performance must be articulated much more clearly so that there is a common understanding by everyone involved as to what is expected. The performance of a team of teams will tend to be tied to the ability of each sub-team to operate successfully. For many large projects, the ability to stay on programme will be governed by the weakest team. I have seen large projects put under pressure by a single team that had started to fail and needed 'rescuing' by other teams working in that phase of the works. Conversely, when every team is working as an effective unit, I have heard of projects surging forward and delivering ahead of schedule. It is therefore worth understanding the factors that have been found to influence team performance.

The starting point is to recognize the distinction between an effective team and a 'work group'. Jon Katzenbach and Douglas Smith, authors of the influential book *The Wisdom of Teams* (1993, p. 45) defined what they called a *real* team to be 'a small number of people with complementary skills who are committed to a common purpose, performance goals and approach for which they hold themselves mutually accountable'. This definition is in contrast to a *working group*, which is simply a collection of people who come together with a shared interest, but no common driving objective. In between there is a *pseudo team*. This is a group who would like to think of themselves as real team, but whose members are not prepared to take the interpersonal risks associated with mutual accountability and the collective action necessary to achieve a common purpose. The word *real* has, however, a different potential meaning that can cause confusion, so I prefer to use the word effective.

The importance of these distinctions is that effective teams deliver results, whilst working groups talk a lot but achieve very little. Pseudo teams quickly devolve to blaming each other for a lack of performance. If a Big Team is one that is made up of many small teams, then the more effective teams you have working on your project, the greater the potential for successful delivery.

Organizations have been searching for the X factor that distinguishes teams that consistently exceed expectations from those that sputter on, sometimes doing well, but then falling into dysfunction. Any firm that can crack the code of team effectiveness is going to have a commercial advantage. The problem has been that teams in a work setting are difficult to study using scientific methods, as there are many potential variables that can affect how a group of people will work together. Finding sufficient sample size is problematic, and so too many studies on teams in a work environment have worked with a limited number of teams. One can find plenty of stories of team performance in military institutions, but the lessons from the Red Arrows or the Navy Seals have limited relevance to the modern workplace. In the armed forces, teamwork can be a matter of life or death, and so huge amounts of time and resources are devoted to team development. Few civilian organizations have the resources to be able to study teams in much depth. That was the case until Google decided to put some serious investment into finding out what makes a highly effective team.

As a business, Google has put considerable effort into finding good people and putting them into an environment in which they can thrive. They have invested heavily in research to understand the factors that will predict a successful team over an unsuccessful one. Charles Duhigg (2016) tells the story of Project Aristotle, where an internal team from Google undertook an extensive piece of research combining both quantitative and qualitative methods to pull together data from 180 teams. Few organizations have the resources or the inclination to conduct such a study. Even fewer would then make the results available to the rest of the world. The output of the Project Aristotle can be found at https://rework.withgoogle.com

The website is a 'must visit' for anyone interested in team effectiveness. As a taster, however, here is a summary of its findings. The research initially focused on the success variables that one might expect including co-location of the team, consensus-driven decision making, individual performance of team members, workload and team size. What is interesting about this study is that whilst each of the above elements obviously plays a part in dynamic of a team, *none* of these variables emerged as a primary driver for success. Duhigg's story picks up on the challenges the initial researchers had in trying to find patterns in the data. What seemed to be a strong feature in a successful team was often also present in a failing team. The breakthrough in the project came when the researchers focused on a team's behavioural norms. Looking at the unspoken rules that governed team behaviour allowed the team to identify five common variables that govern small-team effectiveness:

- Psychological safety – Where team members feel safe enough to take risks and be vulnerable in each other's presence.
- Dependability – Each team member can be relied upon to do their work to the required standard.
- Structure and clarity – Everyone is clear on their own and each other's roles and objectives.
- Meaning – The work done by the team has a purpose that motivates the team members at a personal level.
- Impact – The team thinks its work matters.

These variables should therefore help inform any strategy to create a high-performing Big Team, made up of a collection of effective sub-teams.

Team performance model

This book is structured around a model that is designed to provide those tasked with leading a Big Team with a framework around which to build the different components that are integral to success. Figure 1.2 illustrates the progression of activities that begin in the early phases of a project cycle. In the mobilization zone, performance in terms of output is quite low as the leadership team, and then each subsequent sub-team, takes the time needed to plan how they are going to work as an effective Big Team. Performance then starts to accelerate as the teams move into alignment and begin to learn how to manage the challenges thrown up by novelty and complexity.

Assuming that an effective set-up programme has been implemented, the sub-teams now forming to start the delivery process can begin work in what might be called a *high-performance environment*, which has the following features:

- clear objectives fixed around sponsor and customer needs, giving the team a firm understanding of the desired outcome;
- low hierarchy allowing direct connections between leadership and other specialist teams;
- confidence in a low-blame culture balanced with an expectation of high accountability;
- fluid peer-to-peer networks where teams are encouraged to engage directly with one another to explore solutions; and
- strong behavioural norms that support a collaborative culture.

This high-performing environment creates the conditions in which accelerated learning can take place. I use the word *accelerated* to emphasize the requirement for the teams involved in the early stage of the project to acquire the habits and practices of fast iterative learning.

One of the features of complexity is the impact of too many variables, creating high levels of uncertainty. Fast learning habits allow the teams to explore and experiment moving forward in short bursts of activity and adjusting plans as they go. The team is in effect learning how to learn. Without this period of accelerated learning, team performance will typically improve at a slow but steady pace for a period of time. In a fast changing environment, however, they may not adjust quickly enough to the new conditions and performance, or output is likely to decline.

Performance must then be stabilized at a high level, by keeping the teams engaged and building team resilience. Failure to take action to maintain engagement and resilience will lead to team dysfunction with the subsequent drop-off in performance. There are many other activities that those leading a Big Team must attend to, but these six elements form a basic framework around which to plan and develop how our large project team is going to successfully achieve its intended purpose. This framework therefore sets the structure for the contents of this book.

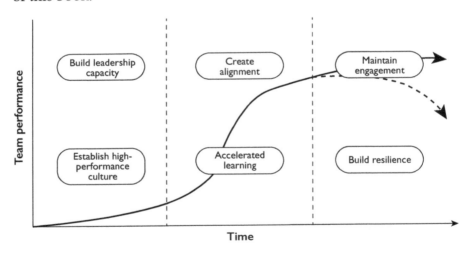

Figure 1.2 Team performance curve on complex projects

Each of the elements identified below is the subject of a different chapter. Chapter 2 looks at the concept of *shared leadership* in large project teams. The underlying theme is that Big Teams don't necessarily need big leaders. We understand the need to be organized and to use the particular strengths of the others in our group. In larger teams, this cohesion has often been achieved in the past by larger-than-life, charismatic leaders, able to align their followers behind them. Increasingly, however, this individualistic 'heroic' style of leadership is no longer applicable, not least because in most big projects the team is made up of individuals from a long and complex supply chain. All teams need some form of leadership, but in Big Teams the ability of a number of individuals to take on the various aspects of leadership at various stages is critical to success.

Chapter 3 looks at the idea of *project culture* and the significant influence that culture has on behaviours. The key to success is to build a culture of alignment, but this cannot be mandated. Instead, the leadership team must create the right conditions to allow the desired project culture to emerge and mature.

Chapter 4 considers the practical steps that teams should take to build *alignment*. Large projects usually begin with a high degree of uncertainty in that whilst the desired outcome is broadly understood, the exact mechanisms required to get there have yet to be conceived. Having many small teams each trying to work out their own interpretation of what will be required it is likely to result in chaos. Big Teams must therefore be able to focus on the right direction of travel even if they are not yet clear on the exact route.

Chapter 5 explores the need to incorporate *learning* as a specific element of team and project performance. Large bespoke projects require the people involved to develop new ways of working that eventually become an established part of that process and procedures. These may be adapted from previous experience on other projects, but even when adopting industry best practice, every major project exists in a unique set of circumstances. The ability of teams to learn quickly is becoming one of the features that distinguishes successful projects form those that stall when conditions change.

The issues surrounding *engagement* are covered in Chapter 6. Human beings are emotionally driven creatures and we are easily distracted, particularly when we do not feel the work we're doing is necessary or important. On the one hand, when we feel positive about our work and have a sense of progression, we will put in additional discretionary effort and creative problem-solving. On the other hand, if we feel remote from the project leadership and do not feel informed about what is happening elsewhere, we can quickly fall into a state of apathy.

Chapter 7 looks at the concept of *feedback* as an essential component of team performance. Without collecting regular data on the factors that impact on performance, leaders and managers have limited information upon which to base their plans to improve how the teams work, both as independent units and as parts of an interdependent network.

The primary issues surrounding *team resilience* are covered in Chapter 8. Major projects exist over an extended time period, often for many years. In the complex and volatile environment in which people engaged in large projects must operate, many problems and difficulties are likely to be encountered. Individuals and teams will find themselves in extended periods of pressure and stress as milestones are achieved and gateways passed. The chapter sets out a framework for building resilience into a team, recognizing that some teams may work through a number of phases in a project, each one exerting different stresses upon its members.

Summary

Team work is a fascinating and multifaceted subject. The book is not intended to be a comprehensive summary of every aspect. My intention is to provide you with a model that you can use to build your own philosophy for leading a Big Team. A philosophy can be thought of as a set of values and principles that set your criteria for day-to-day decision making. Having a clear idea of your own working philosophy is helpful in guiding your own actions and decisions, but if you can then translate the philosophy into a much wider group, it can be an immensely powerful way to build aligned, engaged and resilient teams. Enjoy the journey.

Chapter 2
Leading a Big Team

Humans working in large groups will typically look for someone to guide them towards their common goal. They will listen to those within the group who appear to have clarity of thought to create energy and motivation. We call such people leaders, and a great importance is placed on their ability to guide, organize and inspire. Whilst there is little dispute on the need for this role in large groups, the particular elements that constitute great leadership are more difficult to define.

Any self-respecting commentator on the topic of leadership begins by observing the huge amount of literature that has been already been created around the subject. There are the hundreds of thousands of management books concerned with how to lead other people, along with many millions of web pages. With so much energy and effort devoted to the subject, one would have thought that we would have worked it out by now. Perhaps one of the reasons why so much attention is paid to the topic of leadership is that we are often not very good at it. It is not difficult to find stories of unsatisfactory leadership since the consequences of poor decisions surround us. A cursory glance through almost any newspaper or journal will reveal organizations and individuals who have failed one way or another to fulfil the expectations of their followers.

Of course, much of the literature on the topic of leadership repackages old ideas and presents them from a new perspective. Nevertheless, the thinking on the subject has shifted over the last 20 years. The commonly understood concept of leadership is that it is a set of qualities that is possessed by an individual that allows him or her to perform all of the functions that will direct, motivate and cajole a group of people towards a particular objective. However, as the impact of the complexities of the modern world has become more obvious, there is a growing recognition that successful leadership is less about the individual, and more about the context of the group and how it functions as an effective unit.

So what is the formula for successful project leadership? As yet, no one has been able to scientifically prove that any one particular approach is most effective. Management theories evolve over time, but the continued publication of books and research papers illustrates that, whilst there are many ideas and opinions, no one can claim to have the definitive answer. Perhaps it would be sensible therefore to avoid adding more words into an already overcrowded space. Leadership is, however, a critically important element of success of a Big Team and so this chapter presents my own perspective on the factors that should be considered when designing the leadership framework for a large project.

Leading temporary organizations

The starting point is to understand the entity that needs to be led. As mentioned in Chapter 1, large projects create temporary organizations into which people are managed in a system or structure. Temporary organizations lack many of the elements that act as stabilizing influences on permanent organizations. Over time, each project team develops its own culture but in the early stages of a team's existence, the leadership must make important planning decisions without the security of the cultural precedents that inform the way most permanent organizations function on a day-to-day basis.

The culture of the project organization must consequently evolve, as the early participants decide how they will work together to deliver the commissioned outcome. Culture is important as it heavily influences how decisions are made within the organization and how its members will behave towards each other and the outside world. Project-based organizations usually begin with an objective in mind, but no clear roadmap setting out exactly how to get there. Uncertainty and ambiguity may tempt the project leadership to be cautious in how they design the organization, often defaulting to structures with which they have worked in the past. The danger in such an approach is the likelihood that choices are made that may be appropriate to the smaller-scale projects with which they are familiar, but will be ill-suited to the size and scale of a large endeavour.

As temporary organizations, project teams have an advantage in that they begin their life without the pathologies that reduce the effectiveness of so many permanent organizations. Strategic drift, internal politics, stifling bureaucracy and incompetent management are generally absent when the team first mobilizes. Without strong leadership however, the dark side of human nature draws many large project teams towards dysfunction and potential failure. It is therefore worth understanding how organizational cultures have evolved over the past 500 years, and how this learning can be applied to Big Teams.

Organizational development

In his impressive book *Reinventing Organizations*, Frederic Laloux (2014) identifies the different stages of the evolution of organizations as they adjust to changes in the social, economic and political environments. His thinking builds on studies into the stages of human development and human consciousness by evolutionary and social psychologists such as Ken Wilber, Jean Geyser and Robert Kegan. Laloux's observation is that as human societies develop new levels of consciousness, they are able to make a step change in their ability to collaborate to establish increasingly effective organizations. Using colours to distinguish each stage, he maps how the rationale of people working in large groups has shifted from roaming bands of hunter gatherers, through medieval conformists to the egalitarian, process-based systems of management seen in many of our current organizations. A concise summary of the thinking within each stage is set out in Table 2.1.

Table 2.1 Summary of Frederic Laloux's stages of organizational development

Stage	Description
Red (Impulsive)	Red-stage organizations are typically dominated by a 'chief', where order is maintained by brutal force and the hierarchy is based primarily on fear. Power comes from an implicit threat of violence, and order is sustained through the maintenance of close allies who gain favour by enforcing the chief's will. Behaviour in such organizations is typically impulsive, with limited thought on the implications of their actions

Red-stage organizations are well adapted to chaotic environments such as war zones and failed states, where survival is the principal driver. They are consequently poor at planning and strategizing, being more focused on today rather next year. Such organizations are largely historic, but current archetypes would be criminal organizations such as the Mafia, urban street gangs or the 'warlords' who fill the void when civilization breaks down, as can be seen in war-torn parts of the Middle East or Africa. |
| Amber (Conformist) | Amber organizations emerge from the development of agrarian cultures, as food surpluses allow the creation of more stable societies. A desire for order leads to creation of stratified social classes based around strict rules and tacit codes of conduct. Amber-stage consciousness comes from a recognition that consistent process allows for replication and the ability to take on long-term projects. The use of structure and roles therefore allows for significant growth in scale. However, the |

	world view is static, where things are either right or wrong with no middle ground. Authority now sits within a role rather than an individual, with potential exclusion being used for enforcement rather than physical violence.
	This stage is well suited to stable environments where the future can be planned based on past experience. The underlying belief system is that tomorrow will be very similar to yesterday. Amber-stage organizations consequently struggle to adapt when the environment changes. Behaviours are dominated by a need to be seen to conform to the organizations norms. Amber-stage thinking can still be seen in religious institutions, the armed forces and many universities
Orange' (Achievement)	As cognitive capacity increases, some societies shift to a view where science and the search for understanding have a higher priority. Meritocracies start to emerge and hierarchies are based on ability. Leadership is achievement oriented, focused on solving problems and reaching targets. Dispassionate rationality and task achievement are valued over relationships. The underlying philosophy is that the organization is a machine, where organizational efficiency is pursued at the cost of the individuals involved. Orange-stage culture tends to be focused on single outcomes such as profit.
	Behaviours in orange-stage organizations should be egalitarian and meritocratic with short lines of communication between senior management and operational teams. As these organizations grow in

	size, however, the need of senior management to retain a high degree of control leads to a distortion of the core principles resulting in a lack of congruity between professed values and what actually happens in practice. Orange-stage thinking is typified by the large commercial businesses that dominate the markets in most advanced economies
Green (Pluralistic)	Green-stage thinking emerges from the realization that the orange-oriented focus on material benefits frequently makes them less effective in achieving their espoused goals. The pursuit of profit usually ignores the need to build communities and preserve the natural environment. Green-based cultures therefore seek fairness, equality and harmony through community, cooperation and consensus. Relationships are valued above outcomes, so whilst the orange mindset seeks to make decisions from the top down based on objective facts and expert input, green thinking prefers a bottom-up process that tries to bring opposing points of view together to achieve eventual consensus.
	Whereas orange values decisive leadership, green organizations require leaders who recognize that they are in the service of those whom they lead. If orange uses the language of organization as a machine, green prefers the language of the organism. The preferred view is that different parts change naturally in response to their environment, but that there is a critical interdependency between the different organs that make up the whole of the body.
	Green organizations have a natural dislike of hierarchies and try to empower their employees so

	that decision making is pushed down to the lowest level. Their culture is highly value driven and much effort is placed in delivering positive outcomes to all of the stakeholder groups rather than the mechanistic focus on shareholder profit.

Laloux's argument is that as human consciousness develops, people want to change their organizations to better suit the needs of the wider group, rather than providing a disproportionate benefit to a small number of individuals at the top of the food chain. Whilst Laloux is primarily concerned with permanent organizations, the distinctions between the different colour stages provide a useful mechanism for demonstrating the distinctive needs of large project teams.

Red-stage teams can be quite effective on short-term projects where relationships within the project team are not critical to success. The aggressive 'fist-banging' approach to project management works very effectively if individuals are under performing. Speed tends to be more important than planning, and problems are resolved without the need for much consultation.

Amber-stage teams will be able to tackle projects that have a reasonable level of certainty in terms of required outcome, and a clear route to delivery. In an amber-stage project team, the predominating world view is that the senior leaders are the only people who need to think creatively. Everyone else involved in the project should simply follow the instructions given to them. The presumption that almost every problem can be solved by the careful application of standardized process sits well within the conformist ideology. As complexity and uncertainty increase, however, amber-stage project teams are likely to struggle.

Orange-stage teams understand the need for a higher degree of cognitive flexibility and are more adaptable. They rely less on the strict application of process, but nevertheless place a great deal of faith in the application of scientific principles and the belief that project success can be achieved by adopting a mechanistic approach. Individuals are regarded as cogs in the machine. There is recognition that people need to be cared for, but they are nevertheless seen as easily replaceable. Orange teams are more innovative and are better at holding each other accountable. They are nevertheless prone to place too great an emphasis on targets, milestones and deadlines. Orange-team leadership often loses sight of the human element that is needed to sustain a project over a long programme. These teams consequently lack resilience, and can start to quickly disassemble under extended periods of pressure.

This leads us to *green-stage* project teams who are able to take a pluralistic view, recognizing that both process and people are essential elements of success. Green-team leaders recognize that humans are driven by more than material gain, so time and energy are put into tapping into the need for purpose. There is a strong focus on building commitment and creativity. Green leadership teams are comfortable with ambiguity and uncertainty, and are able to adapt quickly to changes in the project environment. They also understand that control is illusory and consequently there is a high degree of delegation, recognizing the need to pass decision making to those closest to the issue. Green leaders devote a lot of time to articulating and then reinforcing the values that should be adopted. They also careful to pay attention to wider stakeholder concerns.

My purpose in using Laloux's coloured progression of organizations is to illustrate how the leadership of projects must adapt to the prevailing level of consciousness. The relative stability of the late 20th century allowed the conformist top-down approach of amber-stage thinking to work quite effectively. Amber philosophy requires time to plan, design and then deliver. Conditions must be largely predictable, so that every member of the team delivers the output expected to their role but contributes little more. As we have moved into the complex and volatile environment of the 21st century, we are starting to see a tension developing between the polarized belief systems of orange- and green-oriented teams. The orange philosophy of project management still places a high degree of faith in the adoption of systems and process. If a project is struggling, the instinctive belief is that the people involved lack the ability to use the prescribed systems properly. Correction is therefore a matter of changing the people or pushing them to exert more effort. When problems occur, leaders adopt the role of hero, stepping in to 'rescue' the project and get it back on programme (often by working around the systems they have created!).

The process-driven orange mindset understands the need for delegation of decision making, but often struggles to trust subordinates on important decisions. Large amounts of time and money are invested in project controls whose purpose is to monitor as many aspects of the projects process as possible. In practice, however, they frequently fail to deliver any real control as they are too slow to adapt as the project moves through its numerous progressions. The use of heavy-duty control systems illustrate the orange belief that people should behave in the predictable and mechanistic manner that aligns exactly with the measurement systems designed by the project management office. In contrast, the green mindset sees large projects as a set of tasks that require collections of specialists to work together to solve problems that require multiple technical inputs. The predominant philosophy is that people deliver projects, not machines, and that building motivation and alignment to a common cause will generate high levels of productivity.

There is a tension between those two ideologies in that whilst many experienced project leaders understand at a cognitive level that motivation and engagement are important, their training and prior experience leads them to instinctively adopt an orange-stage, process-driven approach. Green leaders put more energy into establishing a clear sense of vision and purpose supported by a well-considered set of values. Vision and values provide the basis for decision making based on principle rather than simply adopting the precedent of what has happened before.

The green mindset acknowledges complexity and the limit that it places on the ability to set detailed plans. Green leaders recognize the futility of trying to impose close control and so invest time early in the programme to build trust between the parties and agree how the constituent parts are going to work together. Establishing a strong sense of real accountability is essential for green project organizations to succeed as they typically reject the coercive mechanisms to bully team members who may be underperforming. Accountability is therefore important for green-stage teams to succeed. It is not, however, a common attribute in many teams as it requires all team members to identify and call to account those who do not fulfil their promises. This is a cultural issue and is typically something that many people working in large projects struggle with.

In a rational world, senior project leaders would consider the environment they are facing and choose an organizational philosophy that best suited the project. The problem is that the shift from orange to green is not based on logic, but on a level of collective consciousness. If your basic belief system is set to command-and-control and a view that process is more important than people, then it is not enough for someone with a different mindset to point out the flaws in your approach. I have found in my research that project teams that shifted to a green philosophy often only did so when they found that the orange-based thinking they were using was not working and they needed to adopt another approach.

My observation is that the default level of consciousness for the majority of project teams working on large projects around the world is achievement orange. My purpose through the remaining sections of this book is to demonstrate that success is more likely to be achieved in Big Teams using the thinking, process and techniques associated with green-stage organizations. I recognize, however, that for some readers, particularly those with a strong process orientation, this may be a difficult journey. Stay with me and you will see that successful green teams also retain process and hard measurement. The key difference is that the mechanisms are designed to support people rather than override them.

JAMES'S STORY

The programme was a multi-million dollar technology project commissioned by a government department in the United States running over seven years. The project had begun with a number of small teams in different parts of the country working on a collaborative basis. As the project expanded, a new project director was appointed who took an 'old school' view on how a programme should run, and changed the way the teams connected by requiring all information and decision making to run through him. He quickly became unpopular with the team leaders of the sub-groups who found his style divisive and overly controlling. Eventually this individual moved on from the team giving the remaining members of the leadership team the chance to reshape how the programme should run.

James, who had been with the programme from the start, worked with a few of his colleagues to explore an alternative approach to leadership. Taking inspiration from General Stanley McCrystal's book *Team of Teams* (2015), they decided to break down the traditional hub and spoke relationship. Superficially, the members of the wider team might not have seen the change as the leadership group, working as a Joint Programme Office (JPO), still functioned as the primary authority within the programme. The critical distinction, however, was the shift in responsibility. The leaders of each of the sub-teams were now required to take on accountability for the delivery of their part of the programme and were given a great deal more autonomy as to how their projects were to be run. By allowing them greater ownership, the philosophy of the programme shifted, so it was no longer acceptable to blame other teams for delays and other issues. Instead, each team was expected to sort out the coordination and collaboration challenges amongst themselves rather than expect everything to go through the central hub.

This shift was illustrated by the change of tone used in programme meetings. The senior team connected in a forum meeting every Tuesday morning and the purpose of the meeting changed from the typical progress reporting session to something much more proactive. In the past, the callers might be complaining they had not been informed of the activities of another group. In the new environment, the group leader would typically explain what had happened in the previous week within his/her team and then ask how this affected anyone else. It was no longer acceptable to complain that you didn't know what others were doing. If you were not aware, then that was your problem and you needed to work harder to keep up to speed.

This shift in responsibility required a change in mindset and not all of the sub-team leaders were able to make the adjustment. Part of the challenge was the need for the sub-teams to recognize the requirement to find the additional resources and bandwidth to remain aware of activities of the wider programme team. It was no longer acceptable to simply exist in your own 'bubble', oblivious to the actions and requirements of others.

By passing down authority from the central hub, the sub-team leaders inevitably began to connect directly with each other, not always keeping the JPO fully informed of their plans and actions. James remembers that this was one of the most challenging aspects of the team-of-teams strategy, as the JPO had to come to terms with the reality that they no longer had control of information flow and needed to accept they did not know everything that was going on in the programme. Instead they had to rely on the fact that they had selected firms and individuals who were experts in their field. The JPO therefore needed to trust that each team would deliver those tasks they had committed to completing.

This new process worked very well for the last few years and the programme is considered to be a success both by its sponsors and the participants. James makes a number of salient points:

- The transition from the old regime took about three months and required the teams to invest time and resources in face-to-face meetings to agree how the new approach would work in practice. There was a degree of 'trial and error' whilst the teams worked out the details of both the philosophy and how it would work in practice. One of the key roles of the JPO became the management of the interfaces between the teams ensuring that there was a consistency of quality of communication.

- Understanding the roles of each of the participants was very important so that is was clear what they could be expected to do and, just as importantly, what they should not be doing.

- The efficient functioning of the progamme required strong administrative support within the JPO. This is a constraining factor for any large project or programme but the distributed authority approach requires good record keeping and event organization at the centre. So rather than being a side role for highly qualified engineers, the JPO employed graduate-level individuals who were more effective in keeping the programme organized.

The outcome has been an ambitious programme that has largely remained on track, hitting key milestones despite a number of changes in senior members of the team both within the JPO and the sub-teams. An interesting postscript is that a new programme director has recently been appointed, and has tried to reintroduce a much more top-down structured approach. This has not gone down well with many of the different leaders of the group and a number of James's colleagues are 'considering their options'!

The components of leadership

The first part of this chapter has made the case that large project teams need to be led as green-stage organizations. This leads to a question as to how the approach to leadership changes when leading a green-stage team of teams. John Sneddon (2003) makes a pertinent observation on leadership in that everyone has their own idea of what leadership means and so we do not bother to clearly define it. He points out that in the same way that 'intelligence ends up being defined by those things that are measured by intelligence tests, leadership ends up being what the various theorists postulate it to be' (p. 102). It is not therefore my intention to put forward a set of leadership rules. Every effective leader eventually works out their own philosophy on the best way to approach the challenge of getting large numbers of people aligned and engaged. My purpose in this chapter is nevertheless to point you in a direction that you may not have previously considered and help you recognize that Big Teams need a distinct leadership paradigm. There is no shortage of advice or opinion on the different approaches to leadership, but, condensing much of the literature on this question, Alan Bryman (1996) believes leadership theory can be broken down into four main approaches.

1. *The trait approach*. A lot of leadership studies have focused attention on the characteristics and qualities that distinguish leaders from non-leaders. Trait theory seeks to identify those particular attributes that could be observed and replicated when identifying and selecting future leaders. In the past, leadership traits used to be evaluated solely on behaviour as observed by others, often based on an imprecise measure of 'character'. In modern times, we have easy access to online psychometric tests and so the process of leadership selection is a little more scientific. Edward Merrow and Neeraj Nandurdikar (2018) carried out an extensive study of 56 project managers who had led large complex projects. Based on interviews, they categorized those who had led successful projects from those whose projects were deemed unsuccessful. They also asked the participants to complete a number of psychometric tests. One of the purposes of their research was to identify the traits of successful project leaders when working in complex environments. They concluded that successful project leaders typically showed the following traits:
   • Higher levels of openness, being prepared to listen to a wider range of ideas and options.

- Lower levels of neuroticism, which led to greater emotional stability, and a greater likelihood they would not avoid difficult issues, particularly interpersonal conflict.
- Higher levels of agreeableness, which showed up in an ability to put people at ease and encourage them to express their opinions.

Merrow and Nandurdikar also tested the emotional intelligence of the participants and found that the more successful leaders tended to score higher on those parts of the test that measure the ability to recognize both one's own emotions *and* those in others. They also showed higher levels of social skills, and were also typically more optimistic.

My purpose in highlighting these results is to illustrate the importance of choosing leaders for large projects whose traits help them become socially capable. These traits paint a picture of a socially adept individual who is comfortable operating in the extensive network of connections that must be made and sustained through the course the project.

2. *The style approach.* The focus here is on how a leader actually behaves. Leadership style can be seen as a particular approach to the role based on the personal preferences of the leader. Style can be both based on a conscious decision, or on unconscious, instinctive choices. Contrasting styles might include transactional styles, laissez-faire styles, assertive styles or democratic styles. Conscious styles are usually developed from previous experiences, formed in our more junior years when working under the direction of an older leader. Most experienced project managers I have interviewed can quickly identify the good and bad experiences in previous projects that have shaped their own leadership style.

3. *The situational or contingency approach.* The approach here is less concerned with the idea of the best way of being a leader and instead focuses on the ability to adjust to the particular

variables that impact a team at any particular period in time. The approach is recognized in the work of Paul Hersey and Ken Blanchard (1982) who put forward a model where the emphasis moves away from the particular choice of style by the leaders, and instead focuses on those who are being led i.e. the followers.

The underlying theory is that the way the leader chooses to act must adapt to circumstances. The approach may need to be dictatorial, persuasive, consultative or empowering, depending upon his/her assessment of the follower's degree of willingness and ability at any particular point. It should be noted that much of Hersey and Blanchard's thinking is focused on individuals rather than groups; it is nevertheless possible to see how this flexibility of approach can work at team, or even project, level. In the context of Big Teams, the situational leadership approach of responding to the needs of different sub-teams, at different times in the project cycle, sits well with the flexible thinking of green-stage leadership.

4. *The transformational approach.* This is an approach where the leader is seen as being responsible for articulating and reinforcing a vision for the organization. This is also sometimes referred to as *charismatic* or *visionary* leadership. The theories around transformational leadership are based on the observation that some leaders are able to shift the mindset of their followers, based on charisma, persuasion, inspiration and vision. Bernard Bass (1990), one of the early commentators on the topic, identified a number of specific attributes of a transformational leader including the ability to find intrinsic motivation, promoting harmony, and encouraging self-management and autonomy. As we will discuss later, these are all important elements to sustaining performance in Big Teams. Ana Tyssen and her colleagues (2013) use the contrast between transformational and transactional leadership to develop the proposition that projects with high and novelty

require greater focus on the motivation of people, rather than a dominate focus on task completion. Whilst the concept of transformational leadership is useful to distinguish the need to focus on people-oriented skills when leading a Big Team, the concept is limited in that it tends to support the idea that great leaders are born, rather than developed. It also reinforces the idea that leadership is a unitary concept where one person leads and everyone else follows.

These different leadership theories overlap and blend into one another, which goes some way to explaining why no single winning theoretical formula has emerged. Each approach makes sense depending on the context of a particular project or scenario. The value in building an understanding of the above approaches is that it can help you begin to articulate your own philosophy or approach to team leadership.

Post-heroic leadership

There is however a significant gap in the above observations in that the focus of much of the literature is based on an assumption that leadership is only carried out by a single individual. As we begin to recognize the difficulties of scale and complexity, the concept of unitary leadership is being questioned. Western culture finds the idea of an individual who can turn adversity into good fortune highly attractive. Our stories portray the leader as an extraordinary individual who possesses a range of worthy attributes that enable him (or sometimes even her) to achieve success where mere mortals are bound to fail.

These stories both reflect and influence how we think about leadership, providing a simple narrative that avoids the necessity to explore the actual detail of a particular situation. Western culture also requires its villains to be similarly handicapped by individual faults and weaknesses that allow us to quickly apportion blame when events turn against us. Keith Grint (2010, p. 83) observes that when things go badly wrong, rather than think through the complexity of the issues, we prefer to find a scapegoat. Looking for heroes (and villains) also enables us to avoid responsibility and to maintain an infantilist approach to leaders that may well have originated with our childhood relationships to parents and equivalent authority figures.

So in selecting leaders, we look for traits, styles and attributes that fit the model of an individual hero, whilst ignoring those that would be more likely to create a 'real leadership team'. If you take the time to explore deeply into the reasons behind the success of large projects, you will find that leadership comes from across the senior members of the team. As Coleman and MacNicol (2015, p. 39) observe, 'whilst we can quickly imagine the single leader who takes on sole responsibility for defining, articulating and ensuring a vision is achieved by single-handedly driving the team forward, this situation rarely, if ever, occurs on projects'.

The recognition that leadership in complex environments requires multiple ownership is becoming increasing understood, as both scholars and managers wrestle with the uncertainties and ambiguities of the 21st century. So, rather than focus on the traits, personalities and leadership styles of particular individuals, more commentators are starting to see leadership as a collective responsibility using the headline terms, *post-heroic leadership* or *shared leadership*. A paper by Lucia Crevani, Monica Lindgren and Johann Packendorff (2007) argues, through a series of case studies, that sharing the burden of leadership not only provides greater ownership of the challenges of leading complex organizations, but also makes the role achievable. Their studies highlight the changing perspectives that take place in a leadership group so that each member of the 'board' sees leadership as a collective constructive process. This implies a shift where leadership moves from a focus on the leader as an individual to a focus on leadership activities. It also moves the focus from leadership outcomes to leadership processes. They emphasize that it is important not to fall into the trap of treating leadership as a theoretical exercise, but instead create a very practical platform for different individuals around the boardroom table to take on the different leadership challenges to which they may be best suited.

Craig Pearce and Jay Conger (2003) provide a comprehensive review of their thinking around shared leadership. They note that in the 21st century, senior leaders are less likely to be asked to work within their professional specialisms and must instead learn how to manage cross-functional teams, where they are no longer a leading expert. In such teams, the leader is at a knowledge disadvantage because his/her specialist knowledge is just one voice around the table, and so he/she must depend upon the expertise of other team members. The other significant change is the lack of hierarchical authority in that whilst the notional head of a large project team has the final decision making power on project issues, he/she will not usually be the line manager of the other individuals around the table. The impact of these shifts in both technical and line management authority is to create a more egalitarian environment.

The point that I am trying to emphasize is that leadership of Big Teams simply cannot be achieved by the individual trying to act as a single primary driver, who is involved in every decision. I am not, however, advocating the complete abolition of a structured hierarchy. Big decisions, especially those with significant implications, need to be owned by a senior group and perhaps ultimately by a senior individual. Big projects will always need someone at the pointed end of the pyramid who holds the ultimate responsibility and accountability to the project sponsors.

From project manager to project leader

When a project grows in size and complexity, basic management is no longer sufficient. The technical mechanics of project management may be adequate for medium-size amber-stage projects. As scale increases to orange- or green-stage projects, leadership now becomes an essential element of the project design. A different set of skills is required, which is a progression in thinking as much as it is a distinct set of capabilities. Michael Watkins (2012) describes the *seven seismic shifts* that a manger needs to make in stepping up from a manager to leader:

- from a specialist implementer of process to a generalist, able to evaluate the wider context of the project's challenges;
- from an analyst of data to an integrator of resources;
- from tactical short-term problem solver to strategist capable of understanding of the 'big picture';
- from 'brick layer' where practical hands-on knowledge is the primary skill requirement to 'architect' designing the systems and operating models;
- from 'problem solver' who takes on the role of hero to 'agenda setter' who recognizes the problem areas and engages others in finding solutions;
- from 'warrior' whose focus sits only within the project team to 'diplomat' who can build influential relationships with sponsor and key external stakeholders; and
- from supporting cast member relying on the guidance and direction of others to the lead role owning ultimate accountability for a successful delivery.

In the context of a major project, these distinctions illustrate the need to develop a new way of thinking about the way leadership works in major projects. Watkins's choice of the phrase, 'seismic shifts' is dramatic, but is appropriate to the message that changes in leadership approach are not incremental. Each of the shifts identified above requires more that an adjustment in technique. Each area requires an aspiring leader to move beyond the simple 'cause and effect' thinking that dominates much of a middle manager's time, and instead see the project from a set of different perspectives. The most important shift is the change in mindset of the newly formed leader in what he/she understands the role to be, and how it should be fulfilled.

The fallacy of control

When designing how your project is going to operate, you would do well to consider the illusion of control. As mentioned, large projects create temporary organizations where authority and power is established by the sponsoring body before the team is formed. Major projects are nearly always a step into the unknown, requiring a large investment of resources, and yet sit outside the sponsoring organization's business-as-usual framework. Where there is uncertainty, humans typically try and reduce risk by attempting to control the environment, usually by imposing a set of rules on the project participants.

The quest for control is endemic within the project management profession as can be seen in the belief that all key activities can be measured, monitored and managed. This has led to a default leadership style frequently referred to as command-and-control. The concept has its roots in the thinking of Frederick Winslow Taylor who published his *Principles of Scientific Management* in 1911. His basic philosophy was that workers should be trained by someone who was their superior, using a 'scientific' approach based on measurement and rules. The exponents of a command-and-control approach to project management are often working under a number of misconceptions:

- Whatever the size of the project, everything can be planned in advance.
- Planning should be done by senior management and execution delivered by workers.
- The transactional processes and procedures designed for small- or medium-sized projects can be scaled up to much larger programmes of work.
- Most problems are foreseeable and can be fixed by the use of risk mitigation techniques.
- Individual creativity, motivation and engagement are not essential elements that should be of concern to management.

If the underlying leadership ethos in red- and amber-stage teams is command-and-control, in orange-stage teams the predominant mindset is 'predict-and-control.' The belief at a senior level is that projects can be planned and programmed in detail, even before a clear delivery strategy has been formed.

This approach might work well if humans were good at prediction, but we are not. We have a tendency to oversimplify the assessment criteria and consequently ignore those factors that either we do not understand or cannot measure. In a complex environment any attempt at accurate predictions of the medium to long term is futile. This is not to say that leadership teams should not spend time planning. The overwhelming evidence from almost every major endeavour is that time spent planning substantially improves a team's ability to cope with unexpected events. In line with the philosophy of green-stage teams, the leadership team sets the direction of travel, and identifies a number of short-term milestones. They are cautious in to making firm commitments that go far into the future. The project environment is periodically reviewed and plans are then adjusted accordingly. The approach therefore changes from predict-and-control to sense-and-react.

Sense-and-react

The sense-and-react philosophy recognizes the fallibility of prediction. Instead of trying to shoehorn task completion into a fixed programme, project leaders work through a continual series of short-term iterations based on the best information available at that time. The process requires a continual scanning of the project environment to assess what is changing and whether decisions need to be adjusted. This requires very good communications between the leadership team, the key stakeholders and, crucially, the teams working at the 'gemba'.[1] The concept of 'sense-and-react' is aligned with the principles of 'agile', where teams work through a series of sprints. Applying agile ideas into the leadership of a Big Team is less about the use of prescribed methods and more about the principle of stepping certainly in a specified direction, but quickly choosing a new route when the current reality interferes with the now outdated hypothetical plans used at the start.

---

[1] For those unfamiliar with Lean terminology, *gemba* is a Japanese term used to describe the place where things happen, or where the work is done. An equivalent British expression would be the 'coalface'.

Regression to command-and-control

It is worth noting that the shift to a green-stage project leadership style can be difficult for those sponsors and stakeholders sitting outside of the project to understand. I have come across a number of examples of Big Teams who have successfully moved to a green-stage paradigm, only to later have a new director put in charge who tries to reassert unitary control.

Schein and Schein (2018) tell the story of a manager at a motor manufacturing company, where a project leader managed to rapidly speed up the design process of a new model by integrating the teams. Rob, the protagonist, had recognized the limitations of the linear process for a design that had so many interdependencies and so he created a 100-person design team. The short-term affect was initially chaotic, but as this large group got to know each other, they started to close out problems very quickly. The interesting part of this story is that a senior executive who had visited the team in action was horrified at the lack of structure and ordered Rob to revert back to the traditional linear processes. Rob apparently said yes to the executive, but then ignored the instruction and carried on using his innovative approach, completing the car design many months ahead of schedule and under budget. The irony in this story is that because the senior executive had demanded the revision to the traditional process, the organization came to believe that it was the use of the linear command-and-control methodology that was behind the success and so the experiment was never repeated.

In another example, Frederic Laloux (2014) charts the progress of a software consulting firm, BSO Origin, which had grown dramatically over a 20-year period based on the principles of openness and trust. The organization worked around the creation of self-managing units, and had virtually no headquarters staff and no staff functions. In time, majority ownership passed to Phillips, a multinational organization, which struggled with the high levels of delegation used by BSO management. They eventually imposed their own corporate control measures leading to a collapse in morale. The subsequent loss of a large number of talented engineers and managers significantly diminished the value of the acquisition.

These examples illustrate a potential challenge for teams that recognize the need to move to a green-stage model. How major projects should work seems to be very much a matter of belief rather than a dispassionate choice of process. The primary factor is whether senior executives and leaders see a large project as a two-dimensional entity that fits neatly into a hierarchical orange-stage organization chart, or a more complicated three-dimensional green-stage model that is mapped as a network of relationships.

When stories emerge of successful teams regressing as a result of a new command-and-control leader being put in place, one can only assume that the new individual feels very uncomfortable with a project ecosystem that cannot be accurately mapped and monitored. I am sure that each of the stories of the reversion from green to orange has some missing points of detail that would help justify their decision to try and reimpose a sense of order. As Laloux comments, when viewed through the lens of a conformist amber or orange mindset, the practices of delegated authority and low control stand out as foolish and even dangerous. In good faith, the board members may feel they are simply protecting the organization by reimposing traditional control-based mechanisms. The problem, however, is that the project team or even the entire organization is likely to then revert to a lower level of performance. Once someone has enjoyed the autonomy and ownership that comes with green-stage leadership it is very difficult to go back to the top-down, command-and-control environment. In every case I have come across, the project quickly lost most of its best managers as they decided to move on.

What do Big Teams need?

The final step of this exploration of Big Team leadership is a recognition that leadership exists to support those people who must deliver the work. One of the important distinctions of Big Teams is their composition of a set of sub-teams, some of which might be Big Teams in their own right. Each sub-team will have a leader who is often the primary connection between the leadership board and the sub-team. These sub-team leaders must be accountable for delivery of that element of the project they have been commissioned to provide. Every major project will have its own particular context, and so the needs of the wider team will differ. They will also change as the project moves through the different stages of its cycle. It is nevertheless possible to identify a number of support requirements that are generic to most large projects:

- Vision – a sense of purpose that can motivate their team.
- Strategic direction – the route map as to how the whole project will play out and where each sub-team fits.
- Cultural alignment – a shared mental model of the behavioural norms that must be common to every sub-team within the project.
- Connections – facilitation of the development of the network within the Big Team. This includes the active creation and management of cross-boundary interdependencies.
- Guidance – support in decision making in times of crisis or uncertainty.
- Data – the collection, analysis and dissemination of key data.
- Stakeholder paradoxes – managing the often conflicting demands of stakeholders.
- Physical environment – where appropriate (and if at all possible), providing the physical space for co-location, project meetings, workshops etc.
- Digital environment – ensuring distributed sub-teams have the appropriate facilities and equipment to be able to easily connect over digital links.

Another way to look at the role of Big Team leadership from a sub-team perspective is to consider what they do *not* need:

- day-to-day direction;
- procrastination and deferred decision making;
- stifling bureaucracy designed for protection of individuals rather than support of the project;
- egocentric behaviour effecting key discussions and decisions;
- continually changing reporting requirements.

The above lists are not exhaustive but are intended to reinforce the point that within a major project, sub-teams should be capable of acting with a high degree of independence, but they cannot operate effectively without support from an effective leadership group. We will consider many of these elements in more detail through the course of this book, but if you look down the list again and consider the work involved in the provision of each task, you can see they are primarily supporting rather than directing activities.

Summary

The purpose of this chapter has been to draw your attention to the distinctive leadership approach required when working on projects that require cooperation and collaboration between a wide range of sub-teams working under pressure in a complex environment. I have tried to emphasize the point that stepping up to a leadership role of a Big Team is not a simple progression of scale, but instead requires a holistic perspective. The team-of-teams structure places a much greater reliance on finding capable leaders throughout the network, who will have the appropriate mix of technical, commercial and social skills to deliver the outputs required of each sub-team. At the same time, attention must be paid to the stakeholders and sponsors who sit outside of the project, maintaining support though regular dialogue. Leading a Big Team is therefore the work of more than one person, and so time invested in building a genuine leadership group that can collectively manage the many interfaces is likely to provide a significant payback downstream.

Chapter 3
Building a culture of alignment

Big Teams require the skills, knowledge and experience of a large number of individuals, who ideally form into a single cohesive collaborative and productive unit. As we have discussed, however, human beings cannot be relied upon to behave in a mechanistic and regimented fashion, preferring to operate in small groups or sub-teams where they can quickly build trusting relationships. In a mechanistic world, each team would behave in a predictable manner, implementing their workload as instructed by senior management. This is not, however, how we tend to work in practice, particularly when trying to create something new or difficult. One of the early challenges for the project leadership is to decide how to bring diverse groups together so that they work effectively, not just on their own element of the project, but critically in the way they support the outputs of the other small teams with which they must interact. The key word in this early stage of a project is *alignment*.

There are a number of facets to alignment. It is obviously a significant benefit to adopt shared systems and process. Similarly, agreeing common approaches to overarching project concerns such as safety or financial integrity are elements that require a degree of consistency in their application. These are nevertheless mechanisms of choice, and will have a limited effect on behaviour between teams. A greater impact comes from the alignment of beliefs and a shared mindset. This chapter looks at the concept of project culture, and how the collective behaviours of groups of people who must work together are steeped in a common set of beliefs as to how their organization works.

Why alignment is important

It is not always the case, but in planning the delivery of a major project, there is a presumption that the leadership will assemble the best people available to them either as individuals or as ready-formed teams from an external supply chain. If the teams are working within a clear delegation framework, one can then also assume that each team is able to decide on the best use of their own time and resources. From a leadership perspective, attention to alignment is therefore concerned with ensuring that each sub-team is also able to make whatever decisions are necessary so that they work to engage and assist *each other*.

It is important to understand that in the absence of a set of positive actions to create alignment, the chances are that many of the sub-teams will start working against each other. The problems of silo working and the tendency for humans to form into competing sub-tribes are discussed in Chapter 6. The point I wish to make here is the need to recognize that big project teams do not naturally follow the patterns of vertical integration that are used in permanent organizations. The sub-teams form, deliver and then disperse. Some will remain involved for much of the journey and can learn to adapt, but many of the teams will arrive with pre-formed assumptions and attitudes. Without alignment, the project can quickly stall as conflict and confusion emerge from a lack of clarity and common purpose.

One way of thinking about alignment is to consider the challenge of leading a flotilla of sailing boats from one destination to another. The fleet may start with a number of boats, which know the desired destination but have no clear map as to how to get there. They are in effect going to have to sail through 'uncharted waters'. The journey is therefore likely to be difficult with many unknown forces to counter and a real possibility of failure. The boats are of different shapes and sizes, captained by individuals with a range of experience, each of whom may have a different idea as to the best route. As admiral of the fleet, your role is to get each captain to point their boat in the same direction. Once the voyage begins, each boat will sail independently of the others, choosing a slightly different path. Viewed as a whole, however, they can be seen to be moving as a collective entity, adjusting their route to deal with troublesome headwinds or unexpectedly strong currents.

The phrase 'team of teams' is a nice piece of alliteration and as such can be easily dismissed as jargon to which one might apply only a superficial meaning. In the context of this book, however, the phrase is important in that a Big Team is not merely a group of small teams working on the same project, but must aspire to become an effective team comprising many sub-teams. To be an effective team requires a common purpose, common performance goals and a common approach. The onus is therefore on the project leadership to be able to articulate just what these common elements look like as well as setting the common framework in which the sub-teams will operate.

Aligning cultures

Any group of people who spend an extended period of time working together will develop their own way of operating that will govern how they behave. This way of working eventually becomes embedded as a set of tacit rules and beliefs that are best described as 'culture'. Discussions on culture within a working environment are generally constrained to its impact within large permanent organizations, and it is not an area often considered in the context of major projects. Whilst project teams may be temporary organizations, they nevertheless still develop their own cultures whose attributes will have a profound effect on the success of the project.

One of the overarching elements of alignment is to influence the type of culture that will emerge as the project team develops. Culture will have a direct and indirect influence on many aspects of the performance of a Big Team, and will have an impact over an extended period of time. From inception to completion, most major projects will be in existence for ten years or more, moving through numerous iterations. The leadership team that begins a major project will probably have different members when it is complete, and the project culture will evolve as the team adapts to changing environments, and different personnel and different stages of the project's lifecycle. How the teams ultimately behave and operate will nevertheless be heavily influenced by the pioneering team whose decisions will shape the project culture at the start.

Yet this topic is rarely discussed by project leaders who are about to start a new project. This is partly because culture is generally not something that is visible. It doesn't fit neatly into a task list or Gantt chart, and whilst team culture can be influenced, it cannot be controlled. Geert Hofstede (1991, p. 5), one of the celebrated researchers in this field, defines culture as 'a collective programming of the mind which distinguishes the members of one organization from another'. The effect of this collective programming is that different groups of individuals working together will operate according to a set of unwritten rules based on social norms, beliefs, values and behavioural patterns. Over time, these elements create a way of interacting within a group that can be condensed into a view as to 'how things work around here'. In existing organizations, both large and small, it is culture that affects how decisions are made, what is seen as valuable and how its members decide with whom they cooperate and with whom they compete.

When working in a group, humans instinctively find a way of fitting in. On first joining an existing group we naturally observe what is happening when people interact, what the others laugh about, what is taken seriously and what strange behaviours seem to be ignored. In time (usually four to six weeks), we adopt the same behavioural patterns as the rest of the group, as this is how we learn to become accepted as part of the group. It is a survival trait that allows us to work cooperatively with others even though we may not necessarily have any close emotional ties to them. As long as everyone follows the same unwritten rules, the group can function as a stable entity. In stable conditions, only those with an unconstrained ego struggle to follow the unwritten consensus as to how the group functions. Groups often develop their own jargon, which helps those who understand it to feel they belong. Culture is also reinforced by the stories that the group tells about itself and its relationship to other groups or tribes. Marcella Bremer (2018) identifies five functions that culture provides for a group:

1. *Collective security.* A cohesive culture provides a group with reduced collective insecurity by creating a shared world view of how things should work. This makes life easier to comprehend and decisions easier to make.
2. *Social hierarchy.* Culture gives people an understanding of position: who are the leaders, who are the influencers and why they have authority in the group. This is a stabilizing feature.
3. *Continuity.* The tacit understanding of how things work around here is usually based on what the group has found to be successful or unsuccessful in the past. Culture therefore provides a way of passing on knowledge and experience.
4. *Identity.* As mentioned above, a shared culture gives humans a sense of identity and belonging. By adopting the predominant styles and behaviours of the group, we become a part of the ongoing story of who the group is and the direction in which it is travelling.
5. *Purpose.* Humans generally form into groups for a purpose, and so when they interact with each other, they reinforce their collective mission around a shared vision of the future.

Having an awareness of these deep-rooted needs will help you shape and influence the culture that you believe is going to be effective for your project. These needs also help explain why behavioural norms can shift if any of these functions are not being fulfilled. The message from the studies of large groups is that cultural alignment is likely to lead to better performance. Bremer points to various research papers showing that firms with strong and cohesive cultures tend to perform above average. Positive cultures tend to create stronger commitment from employees, who report higher levels of engagement and lower levels of turnover. This often flows through to higher customer satisfaction and positive stakeholder engagement. Having a sense of security and teamwork has also been shown to improve innovation and also as being more adaptable and open to change. Cultural alignment is therefore an important aspect of team mobilization, but how can you shape something you cannot see or measure?

Understanding organizational culture

If you want to try and understand or explore the primary elements of organizational culture, there is a range of instruments that have been created by various specialists working in this field. Edgar Schein, Fons Trompenaars, Terrence Deal, Clayton Lafferty and Robin Cooke are among the list of notable experts who have identified an array of different measures that can be used to identify distinct cultural elements. There is a lot of potentially valuable information for an aspiring student of organizational culture to acquire, but for those with limited time, I would point you towards the work of Tim Cameron and Robert Quinn, who have researched and written extensively on the topic. They have created an instrument known as the Competing Values Framework (CVF), which provides a useful mechanism for understanding the different aspects of cultural influence on Big Teams.

The model is based on two dimensions. The first distinguishes organizations seeking order and stability from those who prefer flexibility and the use of individual discretion. The second dimension separates cultures with a strong focus on internal collaboration and unity from those driven by competitive pressure to look externally. The overlaid axes create four quadrants, which can be used to illustrate the potentially competing aspects of cultural influence that will affect how different organizations (and indeed different parts of the same organization) are able to work alongside each other. The model is illustrated in Figure 3.1.

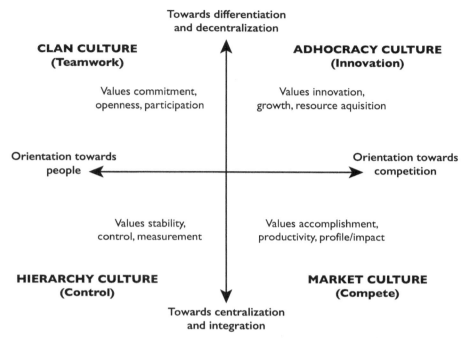

Figure 3.1 Competing Values Framework (adapted from Cameron & Quinn 1999)

Cameron and Quinn (1999) identified how the values will differ for each of the four quadrants, labelling them as Clan, Adhocracy, Hierarchy and Market. The cultural features one would expect to find in each of the segments are set out below.

Clan culture (teamwork)

Organizations that score highly in the upper-left quadrant value flexibility of approach and a strong concern for the internal membership of the team. Clan cultures tend to emphasize openness, participation and discussion. The team matters more than the individual and rewards are based on group performance. Tacit systems are in place to maintain relationships and many decisions will require a degree of consensus. Knowledge is highly valued and resources for personal development are often prioritized. Clan cultures often devolve responsibility, with sub-teams and the individuals within them expected to take ownership of most day-to-day operational decisions.

Adhocracy (innovation)

The adhocracy culture is more outward facing and entrepreneurial, looking for ideas and opportunities for growth and expansion. Flexibility is needed for experimentation, creative thinking and the pursuit of innovation. Leadership is often visionary and is comfortable with uncertainty, and the possible risk of failure. Agility is highly valued and people within the organization are used to continual change. Adhocracy cultures expect team members to be continually interacting with those outside of the project, testing ideas and seeking feedback.

Market culture (compete)

Moving into the lower right-hand quadrant, we see organization cultures that are externally focused but find themselves operating in competitive but predictable environments. The culture derives from the need to survive in crowded markets requiring a continual need to engage with customers to win market share. Making prompt decisions and then quickly taking action are seen as primary attributes. Leadership is often described as hard driving and directive with a focus on short-term results. Project teams with a strong market culture will tend to focus on commercial arrangements and contractual mechanisms for dealing with change.

Hierarchy culture (control)

Hierarchy cultures emerge when there is a strong internal focus combined with a preference for stability. This type of project culture typically values attention to detail and precise analysis. Decisions are taken carefully and there is an underlying belief in the need for logical process. Stability and continuity are achieved through thorough documentation, measurement and reporting. Management is based on hierarchal structures where titles and job descriptions provide a clear delineation of authority and status.

So much for the theory. How does this information help you in understanding how work cultures evolve, and how you might influence the development of a positive culture in your team?

Designing a project culture

If culture is one of the determinants of project performance, it makes sense to put in place a series of actions that, if followed through with conviction, is likely to influence the culture that emerges. The question is less around the type of culture you would prefer and is much more about what you and your fellow leaders believe the project is going to need. Remember that culture is something that develops. It cannot be controlled, insofar as one person cannot control what another person believes. Leaders do, however, have the greatest opportunity to influence how a new team culture forms and is developed. Designing a team culture is not a matter of creating a comfortable and friendly project environment where everyone is helpful and there is no conflict. On the contrary, large projects are very difficult to deliver, requiring many hard conversations and periodically unhappy people. The need is to create a culture where the sub-teams clearly understand their collective goal and believe in the benefits of mutual cooperation. When looking at the future, what cultural attributes do you think will best suit your project?:

- Open or closed: How is information disseminated? What are the political influences on the project?
- Cautious or experimental: What is the team's attitude to risk? Is experimentation to be encouraged?
- Creative or methodological: Is new thinking required, or is it important that the teams follow a prescribed process?

- Financial success or social contribution: Is the driving motive based on the pursuit of commercial profit, or is the purpose primarily to create a better human environment?
- Efficiency or effectiveness: A focus on minimizing cost or investment for long-term gain?

Of course, such choices are rarely that simple, and any discussion on cultural variables will throw up paradoxical needs. Going back to the CVF shown in Figure 3.1, if your project is likely to start with a high degree of uncertainty as to how it is going to be delivered, then logically you would seek to establish the cultural values more associated with flexibility. If you are having to respond to a large number of external stakeholders, you might need a stronger external orientation. Alternatively, you may have a single powerful sponsor who requires order and predictability. If communication and collaboration are important, you will need to develop internally focused attributes.

The reality for large projects is that you inevitably need some aspect of each of these cultural facets. The purpose of the CVF is not to place every organization wholly in one of the four quadrants. An analysis using the CVF framework will typically show a cultural presence in each quadrant, but will highlight a dominant area. The question is not therefore how you develop a culture that is exclusively *clan, adhocracy, market* or *hierarchy* but which of the four will be dominant. In Chapter 2, I made the case for Big Teams to adapt the development of green-stage thinking, which will tend to value many of the cultural attributes of a dominant *clan* or *adhocracy* culture. Orange-stage thinking can be seen in the transactional focus of *market* cultures, whilst the amber-stage mindset will typically be drawn to *hierarchy* cultural values. Problems often arise when these competing cultures clash.

The potential for cultural conflict is illustrated in a study by Raufdeen Rameezdeen and Nishanthi Gunarathna (2003) who used the CVF to explore the high prevalence of conflict in the construction industry in Sri Lanka. Examining the differences between contractors and consultants, they were able to identify strong cultural variations. The consulting organizations taking part in the study tended towards the elements observed in a *clan* culture. Many consulting businesses build their client base through the development of personal relationships, where differentiation is on knowledge rather than price. The culture in such firms can often be summarized by a quote from the senior partner of one of the firms I once worked in. His underlying philosophy was: 'Take care of your clients, take care of your people, provide excellent service, and the money will take care of itself!'

In contrast, the contractors who took part in the research were much more oriented towards a *market* culture. Whilst construction businesses will usually work hard to build relationships with client bodies, large projects are more often than not based on competitive tender, particularly in the public sector. Contractors are typically commercial entities that exist to generate a profit for their shareholders. Working in competitive markets, their primary competence is often seen as a commodity and so margins are therefore relatively tight. Success requires a culture focused on short-term efficiency rather than long-term development.

It would be easy to dismiss the source of conflict between consultants and contractors as a matter of commercial disagreement, but the value of the study was to pick out the distinguishing cultural characteristics of the two groups. The consultants valued loyalty to the organization and teamwork, where the work environment was participative. The contractors valued goal accomplishment, and were comfortable with a confrontational environment where market penetration and production efficiency were the dominant focus of activity. The authors' conclusion was that the cultural differences were so strong that the organizations lacked a common basis around which to communicate in a way that the firms engaged in disputes could understand each other.

Core culture and subcultures

It must be accepted that at leadership level you can only really influence the macro culture of the project. Each sub-team will have its own micro culture. Some of the sub-teams will be new teams built to deliver parts of the project and will be more open to absorbing the macro cultural influences. Other teams will be drawn in from outside of the project, and will arrive with their own macro and micro cultural influences. The question is whether these teams find they have sufficient cultural alignment to be able to work effectively alongside each other, or whether they will be drawn into conflict, as the project develops. Teams with contrasting cultural styles can work together quite effectively in short-term transactional arrangements. If these teams are required to remain engaged over a longer period, then the different values will often create difficulties, which need to be managed.

Where possible, both individual team members, and sub-team units, should be selected, not just on technical and commercial merit but on a degree of cultural compatibility. This is less critical on projects where scope is well defined, and the programme is flexible, but when you need the key members of a Big Team to work as a collective unit, ignoring cultural differences is likely to lead to problems downstream. To be clear, I am not proposing that a Big Team requires total cultural conformity. Each team will develop its own subculture, whatever the wishes of the senior leadership team. Total conformity is not required, or indeed desired, as problem-solving works best when there is a diversity of views around the table.

Vision and values

The concept of aligning everyone in an organization through the use of vision and values statements has become a standard element of senior management practice. Therein lies a problem as too many people have experienced the public announcements of a new strategic plan underpinned by vision and mission statements, which subsequently proved to be meaningless, in that the organization continued to behave in the same way as it had always done. For orange-stage project teams with a focus on predict and control, there is no driving imperative to create mechanisms that will provide directions and motivation. In such teams, there is a belief that planning, measurement and process should be the sufficient mechanisms for ensuring every sub-team knows what it needs to do.

The underlying theme of this book, however, is that the large projects that are being initiated to solve the problems of the 21st century require a contrasting philosophy where leadership provides the framework for success. They must then place greater reliance on the numerous sub-teams to decide how they can best use their specialist skills to contribute to the collective endeavour. This requires green-stage leadership, where the underlying ethos is to operate in the service of the sub-teams. For projects where the precise route to project completion is uncertain at the start, everyone involved needs to have a sense of direction and a set of rules, which tie them together. Having clarity of vision becomes critically important.

Aligning the vision

Projects drive change within organizations, within industries or within societies. The bigger the project, the greater the desired level of change from the current state to a future state. Given the huge amount of resources that need to be committed to large projects, the business case for change usually needs to be quite compulsive. The drive for something better sits at the heart of the vision for a large project. It provides the emotional weight that can unify the different individuals who are going to be drawn into the project and will help provide clarity and direction.

Major initiatives are almost always driven by a human need and so, whether the project is going to fix an old problem or create an entirely new benefit, the outcome anticipated by the project sponsor is to make a group of people better equipped in some way to lead their lives. This is usually the emotional touch point that brings project people together. So the vision for a project is less about the outcomes, of say building a new hospital wing, and more about the number of lives saved or enhanced by having access to better facilities.

When working with multiple sub-teams, you are unlikely to have direct access to each person and so understanding their individual motivational drivers is not possible. Being able to articulate what the outcome will mean gives you the opportunity to align those team members who are motivated by the desire to contribute to something that has a higher purpose.

Aligning values

If the vision gives a Big Team its sense of why it exists, values provide some guiding principles as to how it will go about delivering the project. Values are tied to beliefs and are therefore inherently linked to the concept of culture. A project's values only have an impact on behaviour when they reflect the actions and thinking that the team, or more often its leaders, actually believes are important.

As discussed above, values within existing organizations are often embedded and are not always clearly articulated. For example, an underlying belief that people should always be treated with respect, or that good client service is imperative, does not necessarily need to be written down. In firms that have always worked that way, such values are automatically accepted as informing all important decisions. In organizations where such values have not been present in the past, but are now deemed desirable, they may become part of a change plan and are presented as representing a new set of behavioural norms. They are nevertheless aspirational until time is invested in ensuring the new values become embedded.

In many cases, a major project will start without any embedded values. Whilst certain strong values come across from a parent organization, each major project develops its own culture and, as such, is open to adopting a new set of aspirational values. In the next chapter we will discuss the challenges of deciding on the values that are most likely to influence behaviours in a Big Team. The point to note here is that because values tend to reflect a principle, they are a useful mechanism for helping teams stay aligned, but only when they are interpreted consistently.

Finding the aligning narrative

Another of the cornerstones of alignment within Big Teams is the *aligning narrative*. In the context of a major project, an underlying narrative is the base story that informs the other stories that the teams use to try and make sense of how the project is working. The aligning narrative is neither a catchphrase nor a pithy statement, nor is it a poster on the wall of a meeting room. It is something much more dynamic, which might need replicating in many different formats so that it is absorbed by every single person working on the project. The aligning narrative will be unique to a particular project but common themes might be:

1. This is the situation.
2. These are the challenges.
3. We can only succeed if we collaborate.
4. This is how collaboration is going to work.

The narrative sets the context for subsequent actions, activities and initiatives, which require the sub-teams to build connections and relationships outside their own immediate element of the project or programme. This mechanism is probably one of the most effective ways of connecting people within and across the different sub-teams. It is a proactive management tool that is essential on difficult projects. In the absence of an aligning narrative, people will often start to create their own independent stories, which may push the teams out of alignment. We will therefore return to the topic in Chapter 6 when we consider the challenges of engagement.

Vertical and horizontal alignment

As we have discussed earlier in this book, large project teams cannot be accurately represented on an organization chart, but in reality are a collection of individual units connected formally or informally as a three-dimensional network. Since we are generally not very good at visualizing abstract ideas in three dimensions, there is a need to organize those involved in the project into some form of two-dimensional structure, usually showing the groups with primary authority at the top, with sub-teams grouped into reporting lines that reflect how the project has been set up to provide the appropriate span of control. This traditional method of arranging teams is to a certain extent rooted in the command-and-control philosophy of top-down communication and direction, which in itself is not an entirely negative approach. People are familiar with vertical organizational structures, as they give a sense of place.

The danger of vertical structures is that they form the foundation of 'silos' or 'stovepipes', which lose connection with other parts of the organization. Most managers are used to using a vertical cascade to pass information down the structure, and to collect data, which are passed up. Putting aside for the minute the problems of distortion as messages move up and down the chain, vertical communication channels therefore usually manage themselves. To create an effective network, attention must also be paid to connecting horizontally across the network. This requires time spent understanding where and how communication interfaces need to be established and, in a complex project environment, allocation of resources specifically to smoothing the relationships across boundaries.

Aligning with the money

Another important element that has a strong influence on alignment is money. Large projects are expensive, and are nearly always under pressure to reduce cost. The historical way to constrain cost was to design the output, and then tender the work out to third parties, awarding a fixed-price contract to the lowest bidder. This transactional mechanism remains popular in many industries, particularly those with a high capital cost. What do you do, however, when your stakeholders are in a hurry and want the product or outcome now? Without the time to design and specify what is needed, the procurement process requires finding suitable partners and entering into an arrangement where they are reimbursed, often on a time and materials basis. In such arrangements, costs can quickly escalate out of control, particularly as scope begins to grow.

Too many large projects exceed their original budget, often simply because the initial estimate was too low. More often I have found that huge amounts of time (and therefore cost) are wasted because the different parties are not aligned to the speed of decision making needed to work effectively in a complex project environment. For example, I recently came across a case on a large public-sector contract, where the day rates for a critical specialist sub-contractor needed to be approved by an internal department whose role was to monitor expenditure. In a tight labour market, day rates had risen but the administrator reviewing the proposed rates rejected the contractor's proposal as they were '15% over his anticipated market rate'. The effect on the project, however, was to delay the programme by two months, this being the time it took to go to a higher decision making board for approval. The cost of the labour and overheads for people now waiting to proceed was over £250,000 a month! This is a classic example of the problems of working in complex environments, where existing rules and governance structures designed for a simpler, more predictable world cannot keep up with the pace needed to operate in an agile way.

The money must be right

If a project is to succeed, the money must be right for everyone, not favouring one party at the expense of another. Whilst financial reward is an extrinsic motivator for most people, when it doesn't work, or people feel they are being treated unfairly, then the effect on behaviours can be devastating. My observation is that money rarely has a positive effect on collaborative behaviours certainly over a long period of time. Lawyers and consultants frequently puzzle over the question as to how to establish a contractual obligation on teams to work collaboratively. I have found that as a rule, legal contracts rarely improve behaviour, but badly structured arrangements can have a very negative impact.

If financial incentives are going to be used then they should be as collective as possible. I once reviewed a project where three contractors had been separately appointed to deliver parts of a major roads scheme. Whilst the basis of their appointment was that they would cooperate to deliver the scheme, they were continually trying to protect their individual commercial interests, leading to a projected overrun of a tight budget. Recognizing the futility of this approach, the three contractors agreed a scheme with the client whereby they worked as a collective joint venture and were incentivized to take a share of whatever budget remained unused once the scheme was complete. Having a combined commercial interest now removed the reasons not to cooperate. In forming the joint venture, the management team could now remove many of the obstructive processes designed for self-protection and work together as a single Big Team.

Aligning everyone to the money can be challenging but attention must be paid to this particular issue early in the project. Money may not be an intrinsic motivator, but it is an essential hygiene factor. The leadership team can invest all of the necessary time to establish a collaborative team environment, but if the money doesn't work, teams cannot fully engage. The money can be wrong in a number of ways. It may be that the project is underfunded, but everyone pushes ahead anyway on the assumption that, once started, the project sponsor will have to find the additional funds. Alternatively, contractors may under-price work in the belief that they will be able to extract higher rates from the client when the scope changes. Both of these practices, whilst clearly unethical, are established ways of entering into major projects in many industries. Project managers and commercial managers will argue that projects would not happen otherwise. This somewhat cynical view nevertheless has consequences, as it puts a great deal of stress onto those people who are trying deliver a project in a now hostile environment where collaborative problem-solving is no longer possible.

Aligning with the client

A final element of this chapter I wish to emphasize is the need to ensure alignment with the client or sponsor. Even for organizations used to commissioning portfolios of project work, the task of setting up, governing and then taking ownership of a major project is a difficult and often uncertain process. Sponsors must spend considerable amounts of time, often years, pulling together business cases, gaining support and working through numerous iterations of investment board papers. When the project gets the green light to proceed, they must manage relationships with numerous internal and external stakeholders and then assemble the initial leadership team (ILT), passing over responsibility for turning what began as little more than an idea or concept into a material reality.

Professionals who are used to working in Big Teams can often allow themselves to become disconnected from the client/sponsor, particularly when the sponsor has limited practical knowledge of the technical delivery process. On major projects, the client may recruit their own specialists to watch over the project and ensure that the proper governance procedures are followed. The danger for the project team is they fall into a formalized communication routine, and lose connection with changes occurring in the organizations that sit outside of the project bubble. When the project comes under pressure, it is all too easy for the client to become seen as an opponent to the project team rather than a supportive advocate.

One of the elements of project success is to create and maintain strong personal links with the sponsor, be they an individual or a group. It is important that everyone understands from the start the challenges ahead, and that the best way to get through them is to work together in a mutually supportive relationship.

Summary

Do not underestimate how difficult it can be to get the different parts of a Big Team into alignment. Perhaps one of the biggest mistakes a new leadership team can make is complacency. People can be difficult, unpredictable and messy. They can also be creative, committed and industrious. How they turn up to work on your project will be heavily influenced by the environment that they are required to work in. The next chapter will consider some of the activities which, when applied the right level of energy and consideration, will align your sub-teams and set the project off in the right direction.

Chapter 4
Team set-up

Having established the need for all of the parts of a Big Team to face in the same direction, we should now explore the practical process of establishing alignment of the numerous sub-teams that will be joining the project over the course of the programme. This chapter works through the different components that should be considered in the early stages of the life of the project team.

The set-up process can be thought of either as an investment process or a risk management exercise. From an investment perspective, spending time building strong interpersonal relationships at the start will enable each team to work as an effective and cohesive unit. The same principles also apply to relationships between teams that are dependent on each other to deliver their respective components of the project. Incurring costs on activities that do not, at least initially, appear to be directly connected to technical delivery can be unsettling, particularly if you are under pressure from sponsors to show early progress. There is, however, a great deal of truth in the old adage that 'failing to plan, is planning to fail'. In the context of a successful Big Team, planning in the early phase of a project should be less concerned about 'what we are going to do?' and more about 'how are we going to work together?' This is an important distinction because too many project leaders make the flawed assumption that professional people will naturally be able to connect, communicate and collaborate with others on the team.

This leads us to the question of risk management. All large projects are going to encounter unforeseen problems that can lead to conflict, the costs of which can be huge when they upset the team's dynamics. This is obvious when teams become bogged down in commercial disputes, which can disrupt or even halt progress. Less visible is the damage caused by a lack of problem-solving, linked to low levels of trust, where decision making must be passed up and down the management hierarchy, creating delays. The studies on effective teams often highlight their ability to make steady progress, finding answers to problems together without requiring senior management attention. Putting in place the processes that build trusting relationships will therefore significantly reduce the potential for delay and disruption downstream.

Stages of team development

Before we consider the different elements of the set-up process, it is worth reviewing the research into the different stages of team development. Many students of project management are aware of Tuckman and Jensen's (1977) stages of small-group development. Their observations that new teams go through a process of forming, storming, norming and performing has rhyming element that is easy to remember.

Bruce Tuckman initially devised this model back in 1965, and it remains the most widely recognized structure for the development of small teams. Inevitably the model has come under a degree of criticism in the following years. Tuckman himself identified a lack of quantitative rigour in his observations, and much of his initial work was focused on therapy groups rather than teams working in commercial organizations. The model has nevertheless remained as a reference point for researchers in this field. It is not, however, the only group-development model. Levi (2017) identifies three other possible theories of team development, which are briefly summarized in Table 4.1.

Table 4.1 Alternative theories of team development

Author	Development stages
McIntyre and Sales (1995) (based on skills development)	Stage 1 – Clarification of roles Stage 2 – Coordinated skills development Stage 3 – Increasing the variety and flexibility of its skills as a team
McGrath (1990) (for project teams)	Stage 1 – Inception. Focused on planning and collaboration activities Stage 2 – Conflict resolution as social relations become strained Stage 3 – Problem-solving. Focus on coordination of roles and actions Stage 4 – Execution
Ancona[1] and Caldwell (1990) (for new product development)	Stage 1 – Creation. Focus on a mix of internal processes and external relations, building resources and making connections Stage 2 – Idea development. Internal focus on the technical details of the project Stage 3 – Diffusion. Refocus on external relations and transfer to manufacture and marketing

Most commentators recognize that not all teams will follow the same routine of stage by stage development. The purpose in setting out some of the theories around development is to show that, whilst models and theories may differ depending upon the circumstances, every team must move through some form of sequential development. The error made by too many team leaders is to try to either speed up or even skip the early development stages and move quickly into delivery. The overwhelming evidence is that such an approach usually leads to underperformance. People working in teams need to go through a socialization process as it allows them to learn to understand and trust each other. The message is to be patient, and use the early stages to ensure the team emerges with strong and positive behavioural norms.

Aligning behaviours

The one factor common to all the sub-teams involved in a large project will be an internal pattern of behaviours, which is shaped *but not fixed* by its culture. As we have discussed, behaviour is a multidimensional phenomenon that cannot be controlled but can be influenced, particularly when a team is newly formed. Project teams often display a degree of uniformity in their behaviour, usually as a result of a strong influence from the leadership team. This uniformity may be positive or negative. Some teams learn quickly how to establish good relationships and resolve problems between themselves without the need for continual escalation. More often, however, one finds that once a project begins to encounter difficulties, behaviours become dysfunctional, communication is formalized and collaboration ceases. This scenario will be familiar to many experienced project managers. It has often surprised me how many project professionals have come to regard a dysfunctional project environment as being the norm. Project leaders should therefore regard the challenge of establishing collaborative behavioural norms as one of the most important tasks in the project cycle. This is true for a team of any size working on a complex project but in a Big Team it is the secret to building true alignment. In the sections below, I have set out a series of activities that have been shown to have a significant impact on how teams work together. These activities have been found to be effective because they provide the psychological foundations upon which a team can first build and then prosper.

One of the fascinating aspects of human behaviour is that a new set of behavioural norms is formed every time a new group comes together. Once behaviours in a group are set, however, they are often difficult to change. The team's set-up activities must therefore be planned into the start of each part of the programme when a new team is formed. This is often inconvenient as most projects begin with a high sense of urgency, partly driven by the sponsor, but often by the desire of technical people to get started on the technical tasks they believe they have been assembled to deliver.

Most of the successful large projects I have come across in recent years have featured a leadership team that recognized the need to slow down and take the time needed to get the key parties, including the sponsor and major stakeholders, into alignment around *how* they would work together. My own experiences are supported by Merrow and Nandurdikar (2018) who caution against project teams being overly 'schedule driven' in the early stages of a project where the management team becomes almost solely focused on working out how to hit a set of pre-agreed milestones. They refer to the term 'front-end loading' (FEL), which they define as the process by which a project is conceptualized, developed and defined prior to the start of execution. In their study of 56 project managers experienced in leading major projects, they found that those project leaders who used the FEL period to take a holistic view of the project were much more successful, particularly where time was spent focused on stakeholder- and people-oriented issues. It is interesting to note they also found that where FEL time was cut short in response to programme pressure, mega projects nearly always failed to deliver to expectations.

THE ARROGANCE OF PRESUMPTION

In the course of my research I heard a story that contains many elements of the problems created in new teams where time is not invested in establishing strong social norms. A team had been assembled to design a technically sophisticated production centre for an international company. The project was to be the first of a series and so offered the assembled team the prospect of an attractive pipeline of future work. The individuals were all very experienced, but had never worked together before. The sponsor had arranged a team familiarization session and had brought in an external team coach to run the session, which was scheduled to last a full day. The agenda was set to cover a number of the important socialization activities such as agreeing common objectives, effective communication and team behaviours. Shortly after the first session began, one of the participants began to object, stating that the session was wasting time. The gist of his argument was that everyone around the table was an experienced professional, and they did not need to learn how to work as a team. The others around the table agreed, suggesting the facilitator change the agenda to focus instead on technical task planning. The project sponsor lacked experience of dealing with a senior group and succumbed to the pressure to change the nature of the workshop. The result was that no time was spent agreeing a common basis for working together.

The project began with many gaps in scope as there was pressure from the company's board to deliver the facility to a compressed timescale, and quickly fell into difficulties. Within three weeks, two of the sub-team leaders had fallen into dispute over a relatively straightforward issue, and were complaining to the client about the other party's behaviour. The first monthly leadership team meeting went badly as arguments broke out over who was supposed to take responsibility for a number of relatively minor tasks that were not covered in the original brief. Rather than becoming a team, different individuals had taken entrenched positions that slowed the progress of the project. Instead of accelerating into the design process, the group formalized all communications through the project manager, as each party now became concerned about protecting its own interests. The environment settled into a stilted set of behavioural norms where each part of the design team carried out what they saw as their own contractual obligations, but offered limited cooperation to their counterparts in other teams.

The design phase, which should have lasted 20 weeks, extended into the delivery phase of the project. Under pressure to remain within the original programme, delivery contractors were appointed with an incomplete design. On joining the project team, the new members quickly picked up on the dysfunctional behaviours and immediately adopted similar norms. It will not surprise you to learn that the project ended over time and over budget. None of the participant firms was invited to take part in the next phase of the programme.

The question is whether there would have been a different outcome if the team had invested more time at the start. Perhaps the egos of some of the primary antagonists would have always created problems. However, had the senior group worked through the socialization processes, they would have identified the warning signs and the trouble that might lie ahead. The project manager and the sponsor would also have had the social contracts in place that would have helped them tackle the communication issues much earlier.

Set-up methodology

Whilst it is true that some teams assemble slowly as a project builds momentum, most project teams go through some sort of start-up phase where a senior team meets to plan the work ahead. As discussed above, the tendency is to focus much of this valuable time on task planning rather than social development. Having established that this early part of a team's lifecycle must be devoted to building trust and cohesion, it is useful for a Big Team to use a consistent model of team development. In the sections below, you will find a team set-up framework with eight primary components:

1. Articulating a compulsive vision
2. Actionable values
3. Testing assumptions
4. Building 'Level Two' relationships
5. Establishing the team rules of engagement
6. Clarifying roles and accountabilities
7. Agreement of the management of conflict
8. Recognition of the need for iterative learning

The first team that should work through the set-up process described above is the ILT, i.e. the leadership group that is assembled to begin the project. The output from these sessions will establish a set of 'core principles' that will establish how they see the project playing out, and how the teams will work together. This is a time-consuming task that should take several days. If this seems a long time to spend, remember that the payoff downstream will be substantial. My recommendation is that for major programmes, the ILT should engage a facilitator experienced in team coaching who can help shape the discussions arising from each of the set-up exercises and ensure that the output from each session is written up and disseminated.

This is a framework rather than a prescribed process. Each element, where given the proper attention, has been found to have a strong influence on team development. However, every team is different and so the set-up process will need to be adapted to their needs. The framework nevertheless provides a starting point upon which each team leader can build their own bespoke set-up plans. The point of having a prescribed framework is that to build alignment every sub-team should go through a similar, if not identical, process.

1. Articulating a compulsive vision

In Chapter 3 we considered the importance of having a vision for the project team that would form the basis for aligning each of the sub-teams. This is one of the first tasks for the senior leadership team to consider. Michael West (2012, p. 111) defines a team's vision 'as a shared idea of a valued outcome which provides motivation for a team's work'. A clear vision will help make sense of the strategic decisions, which will frame how they work. The challenge is to be able to explain the vision in terms that will not only make sense to the sub-teams, but will also provide them with the 'guiding star' that helps keep them aligned. It is useful to explore just what the impact of the project is going to have when it is complete. The following questions may help the vision emerge:

- What will the project change?
- What is the desired economic impact?
- What is the desired social impact?
- How will it affect the lives of the people who use it?
- How will it impact on the lives of people around it?
- Who will be happier/healthier/safer?

The process of articulation of a clear vision is not always easy. Finding the messages that will convey the intended meaning may take time. Whilst it is potentially very helpful to find a vision that is motivating to a broad audience, the most important factor is to help those people directly engaged on the project make sense of why they are part of this team of teams.

At the start of a major project, the ILT team have a limited idea of just who they are going to be communicating to as the full team has yet to be assembled. Furthermore, people will be motivated by different drivers. I have interviewed people who were genuinely inspired by the impact their project was likely to have on the wider community. For others, particularly with those of an engineering mindset, motivation came from being part of a significant project. The ILT team must therefore find the best way they can to explain their vision in words, and even in images, that will make sense to different mindsets.

When articulating the vision, the pioneering team need to anticipate that their output will then be passed over to each sub-team, who must then consider the vision and spend some time discussing the question 'so what does this mean to us?' Every sub-team is consequently likely to have their own interpretation of the vision, which might seem to negate the value of trying to find a single coherent message that binds the teams together.

For more ideas on building out the vision see http://teamcoaching toolkit.com/toolkit/compulsive-vision/

2. Actionable values

As discussed in the previous chapter, values are the primary element that will shape the culture of a project. Every member of a newly formed team will arrive with their own embedded values, whether they are personal or organizational. A major project is nevertheless a unique enterprise that will develop its own values. An early task for the ILT is to articulate and then embed a number of explicit values that will set the project on a successful trajectory. This is an exercise that requires some thought.

As a new organization it is useful to start with the premise that there are no established values. Whatever culture is to evolve will therefore depend upon those values that are to be defined, agreed and articulated. The challenge with this exercise is to avoid falling into the 'so what?' trap in which a set of values is chosen that makes little material difference to the way that the sub-teams behave. The answer is to focus less on what happens within each of the sub-teams, as they will each evolve their own subcultural values for what goes on *within* their team. Instead, the thinking should explore those cultural behaviours that affect interactions *between* the sub-teams as these will have greater overarching influence.

I have noticed a tendency for leadership teams to choose values that are worthy, but are nevertheless quite ineffective. A common example is to choose a value of 'respect'. What exactly does this mean in practice? Is it about being polite and moderating language to avoid causing offence? And if everyone is respectful, what difference will it make to the project? More importantly, what actions does one try and put in place to create an environment of respect? Another example is 'integrity'. Why would anybody engage with an individual or firm who lacked integrity? There are certainly going to be situations where teams act in a way that might be deemed by others to lack integrity, but the team itself will usually be able to argue either that it was acting in good faith or was merely reacting to the lack of integrity shown by other parts of the team.

If you look at the values statements of a range of large organizations you will often find that half of the words chosen are meaningless insofar as they have few mechanisms to actively influence behaviour. To be clear, I am not claiming that respect and integrity are not important. They are essential attributes of team behaviour. I therefore see them as inherent characteristics that are part of the price of admission to the Big Team. Few people would choose to work with anyone with a reputation for low levels of integrity or who consistently showed a lack of respect. In a networked world, organizations, and to a certain extent individuals, that display such behaviours quickly gain a reputation and are unlikely to be invited more than once to participate in a successful team-of-teams environment.

There is a school of thought that says one should have no more than four explicit values, on the basis that beyond that number the impact of the values statement becomes less effective. The pioneering team should focus on the best four actionable values they aspire for the team. Whatever words are chosen must therefore be capable of practical implementation. Words that can often be found in project values statements such as openness, innovation, safety or transparency may be valid and appropriate to the proposed scheme. To have an impact, they must pass the 'so what?' test. A useful example is collaboration, since this is ultimately one of the underlying behavioural elements most likely to lead to effective problem-solving. The questions the ILT must answer before committing to such a word or phrase are:

1. How will collaboration actually work?
2. What would good collaboration look like?
3. What can be done to encourage collaborative activity?
4. How will we measure that it is taking place?
5. What might be done where it is not happening?

Working through these questions will help you explore the practical implications of the values that have been chosen, so they can then make a positive contribution to the creation of a high-performing team environment.

3. Testing assumptions

One of the benefits of pausing to take time to think is to identify potential problems ahead that may not have been considered in the often disjointed process of getting the project to the 'starting line'. Projects often begin in what Michael Cavanagh (2012) describes as a *conspiracy of optimism*. His observation is that in their desire for a project to happen, many of the primary participants choose to ignore potential risks and push ahead in the vague hope that everything will somehow sort itself out. It is therefore a useful exercise to consider what assumptions the ILT might collectively be making, now the commitment to proceed has been made. This desire to press ahead without checking the conditions can lead the sponsors and other early participants to make a 'leap of faith' where a decision to proceed has been made despite evidence that should prompt a more cautious approach. To paraphrase the 20th-century comedians Laurel and Hardy, the pioneering team needs to consider 'what sort of mess have we gotten ourselves into this time?'

Many projects begin with incomplete information, requiring those responsible for planning the project to make a number of assumptions as to how the anticipated programme will play out. An assumption can be defined as a thing that is accepted as true, or as being certain to happen, without proof. Some assumptions are consciously made and the associated risks noted. There are other assumptions, however, that have a less conscious basis. Assumptions are recognized as a cognitive short cut, where we subconsciously decide not to think in any depth about a particular aspect of an issue or problem. Assumptions often tend to be based on a past experience without considering all the factors that influenced that event.

The key question that the pioneering team should address is 'what has to go *right* for this project to proceed?' It is important to note this is very different to the question as to what could go wrong. There are hundreds of permutations of problems that could occur. The question as to what needs to go right is much more focused on the conditions in which the project must operate. A good way to address this problem is to divide the question into its technical, commercial and social elements. The technical and commercial discussions may be illuminating and will probably throw up a number of further questions that will need to be researched. The question 'what has to work *socially* for the project to proceed?' should however get the team focused on the specific challenges of how the people engaged on the project will interact, both with each other looking inwards and also with those looking outwards. Some common flawed assumptions include:

- The client/sponsor is equipped to make all of the decisions needed to keep the project on programme.
- Budgets are securely funded.
- The primary stakeholders will continue to support the project.
- Key players involved in each stage of the programme have the competence and resources to deliver on their promises.
- Once assembled, the sub-teams will collaborate to solve problems.

The reality is that once the decision to proceed has been made, there is probably little that can now be done to change the course of action. Budgets and deadlines have been set and it is the pioneering team's role to work out how to deliver. The purpose of the exercise is to shake out any complacency that may exist. Once the team recognize the potential level of difficulty they face, it should then encourage them to take the process of effective team set-up more seriously, putting the time and thought needed to overcome the potential hurdles that are now likely to arise.

4. Building 'Level Two' relationships

One of the lessons learned from the various researchers into the performance of large projects is that Big Teams will succeed or fail depending upon the quality of the relationships that exist throughout the team. Most people would agree that this statement makes sense, but what does it mean in practice? In their book *Humble Leadership*, Edgar and Peter Schein (2018) offer a simple but easy-to-apply model that helps explain the type of relationships we should be seeking. They identify a relationship continuum that comprises four levels as shown in Table 4.2.

Table 4.2 Relationship levels (adapted from Schein & Schein 2018)

Level Minus One	Level Minus One represents master–servant relationships based on total impersonal domination and coercion by one person over another.
Level One	Level One identifies transactional or bureaucratic relationships tied to role- and rule-based supervision or 'professional' interaction. Such relationships are impersonal and dispassionate.

Level Two	Level Two relationships are personal, cooperative and trusting relationships where we see others as human beings, acknowledging the whole person.
Level Three	At Level Three, relationships become emotionally intimate, with strong mutual commitments.

The Scheins define a relationship as *a set of mutual expectations about each other's future behaviour based on past interactions with one another* (2018, p. 22). Their argument is that for humans to work effectively together, they need to engage based on Level Two relationships where there is some symmetry in the confidence and trust that each person in that relationship can have in the other. Without symmetry, the relationship will remain transactional or will even end.

Few leaders in a work environment would acknowledge they allow Level Minus One relationships to exist in their organizations but they can nevertheless evolve where one person has a high degree of power over another who by force of circumstances must accept the dominance of a manager or supervisor. The underlying theme of Schein and Shein's book is that the default position taken in our day-to-day work is to settle with Level One relationships. At Level One we may know the name of the other person and the role they are performing, but know little more about their lives. We complete our transactions with them and move on having little emotional concern to their future success or failure.

To work effectively together, the Scheins argue that individuals must move towards Level Two relationships, where we have a greater level of knowledge of the factors that shape the lives and behaviours of those we work with on a regular basis. When we have a greater degree of understanding, we accept others for what they are as human beings rather than simply identifying them with the job they do. We are consequently more able to build the trust and friendships that are a critical component of high-performing teams.

Enabling and encouraging Level Two relationships throughout the team is therefore one of the tasks that should be owned by the leadership of every sub-team engaged in the project. For those who like the idea of continuous progression, it is worth pointing out that Level Three relationships are close and intimate and tend to be limited to very strong personal friendships. Whilst such relationships may evolve over time, they are not part of the responsibility of a team leader. The focus should therefore remain at Level Two.

As with so many aspects of group culture, the level of relationships we aspire to will be shaped by the behavioural norms of the group. If all we see around us in a particular group environment is transactional Level One relationships, then we will not make the effort to move to Level Two. In a Big Team environment, it is important to establish as part of the set-up process that learning about the lives of those people with whom you are going to regularly interact is an important task.

How team members learn about each other is to a certain extent up to them. Some are naturally gregarious whilst others may feel reticent to reveal personal information. However, if you have established the cultural norm that everyone talks about the issues that affect their wider existence, it becomes socially acceptable to take time to discuss what happens outside of the narrow constraints of a particular role.

There are numerous different ways to encourage the development of Level Two relationships. Anything that involves social interaction outside of a work-related meeting is going to help. Whether it is a formal meal or a trip to the local pub after work, encouraging your team to meet in non-work environment will help. Such informal meetings work well when in small groups. Taking a large group to the pub may be less effective in that when forced into a social situation with a lot of other people we do not know, we will clump together with those we already know.

Building Level Two relationships is sufficiently important not to be left to chance. I would therefore advocate the use of more structured approach. The task is not usually difficult. It is simply a matter of giving people time to ask questions of each other. For example, I recently acted as an observer for a project kick-off meeting for a large station redevelopment project. The event would be the first time that the client's team and the newly selected contractor's team would meet each other. A three-day off-site meeting had been arranged, which would cover a range of planning activities but was principally designed to help the two groups get to know each other before forming an integrated leadership team.

A venue was chosen that would require the attendees to travel by train on a journey that would take just under an hour. Each person was given a ticket and reserved seat that would sit him or her next to their counterpart. In their instructions for the journey they were given a set of questions to ask each other. These questions ranged from the professional to the personal. When they arrived at the venue, each person was then required to tell the rest of the team what they had learned. This proved to be a very effective way of introducing the team to each other in a way that started with the whole person rather than limiting any formal discussions to their immediate role.

Patrick Lencioni (2005) suggests pushing the boundaries a bit further. He sets out an exercise specifically designed to build trust by getting people comfortable with moderate vulnerability. He calls it a Personal Histories exercise, which requires a small group to go around the room where each member must explain three things: where they grew up, how many children were in their family and what was the most difficult or important challenge of their childhood. Importantly, this is not about their inner childhood, just the most important challenge of being a kid. Lencioni comments that whilst he often feels unsure as to whether this exercise will work, he continually finds that the process produces information that surprises the others in the room and helps build an acceptance of vulnerability.

I pick these two examples to illustrate the different levels from which you can approach the task of building strong relationships. Whoever is designing the exercise must make a judgement call as to how 'deep' to ask the participants to go. I would urge you to be brave. Teams who are able to work through stories that stir emotions bond much more quickly and are more likely to work as a collaborative unit. I was told a story of a team who were working through a variation on the Personal Histories exercise, when one of the group decided to reveal an emotional story of the severe hardship he had worked through in a previous role that had threatened his professional existence and ultimately his physical health. The story was uncomfortable for the group to hear, but they listened, acknowledged and sympathized with the storyteller. This group went on to form a highly cohesive and productive unit outperforming all of the other teams engaged on a lengthy refurbishment programme. When asked how they became such a tight team, many of the members credited that workshop as the moment they began to bond.

5. Establishing the team rules of engagement

As we have discussed, every group will establish a set of norms that will govern those behaviours that are deemed acceptable and those that are not. Unless the norms have been articulated, these will remain tacit and largely unspoken. One of the problems for any group is that without positive guidance, behaviours will quite often deteriorate over time. Humans will inherently seek to preserve energy or to take advantage of opportunity. The consequence is that we may become lazy and less conscious of the need to work in harmony with our co-workers. For example, some people start to turn up late for meetings, or spend time staring at their phones rather than focusing on the discussions at hand. Egotistical behaviours begin to emerge and the team starts to underperform.

To counter this tendency towards dysfunction, each team should be encouraged to establish their own set of ground rules, often called the 'rules of engagement'. These rules essentially set out how the team will operate when they meet and how they communicate outside of meetings. This is a process of co-creation where every member of the team feels involved in the process. The exercise might ask questions such as:

- What do we expect from each other?
- How should our meetings work?

- What does good communication look like?
- What are the behaviours that will help us succeed?

Such discussions allow a set of principles to emerge that can then be summarized as set of 'rules'. These should be written down and each team member asked to verbally state their agreement (or otherwise). This process establishes a contract between team members and provides a basis for holding each other accountable.

Some organizations may see this exercise as creating a 'team charter'. Whilst there may be some overlap, I have found many team charters to contain numerous other aspects of a team's protocol including vision and mission statements, roles and responsibilities, budget and resources, and so on. This is not necessarily a negative, in that any activity that helps the team acknowledge its social commitments is likely to have a positive effect. My problem with such documents, however, is they often become slow to produce and bloated with too much content. The thicker the document the more likely it will gather dust in a filing draw. My preference is for a short, visually clear document that provides the team with the mechanism to pull each other back into line when they start to become lazy or complacent.

For further ideas on setting your team's rules of engagement check out http://teamcoachingtoolkit.com/toolkit/establish-rules-engagement/

6. Clarifying roles and accountabilities

Most people believe they are familiar with the concept of 'roles and responsibilities' and the idea that each member of a team has a distinct role, the outputs of which should be clear to everyone else. I have found very few teams, however, where there is absolute clarity on the team's roles. When pressed, most team members are unclear exactly on the boundaries their own role, never mind the roles of others in the team. It is not therefore a surprise to find that one of the most common complaints from teams when giving feedback is that roles lack clarity. Investigating these comments further usually highlights two distinct issues:

- Authority – which roles have authority over me and what authority attaches to my own role.
- Voids – who is going to deal with the tasks that do not appear to attach to anyone's current role in the team.

In an effective team, both of these concerns are generally absent, in that the essence of a real team is to solve these problems amongst themselves. Authority is less about instructing others or having the first claim on team resources. Instead, authority sits with the team as a unit where the focus is fundamentally on what must be done to achieve the collective goal. The same principle applies to voids, or gaps, in the team's roles. Strong teams fill the gaps by dividing unfilled roles amongst themselves until additional resources can be found.

With the above observations in mind, every new team should take time at the start to discuss the question of roles and who is going to take ownership of particular tasks. These discussions should quickly move beyond the technical disciplines of the men and women around the table. Much of a project team's workload will sit within particular specialisms and so there is little debate on who should own technical tasks. The gap in most teams is to agree who will own the informal tasks that build the team environment and take care of the numerous issues that sit outside of the technical specializations.

Responsibility vs accountability

The phrase *roles and responsibilities* is another piece of alliteration that rolls easily off the tongue. It has become a stock phrase whose actual meaning has been diminished. Role descriptions are usually prepared by listing the tasks that are done when performing that role. It is the completion of these tasks that therefore establishes ownership or responsibility. Responsibilities are effectively the output. The problem for the rest of the team, however, is that output and outcome are not necessarily the same. Too many role descriptions therefore focus on activity involved in the role rather than setting down the outcomes the role is meant to achieve. This is where accountability comes in. Dictionary definitions are not very helpful in separating responsibility from accountability and all too often the words end up being used interchangeably. The team should therefore focus their early discussion on how true accountability will apply and to set the expectation that they should hold each other to account. For teams engaged in project work, what ultimately counts is handing over an element of the project complete and ready for its next stage. From the perspective of the wider team, it is the effective completion that counts, rather than the processes undertaken to get there.

A practical suggestion as to how to create an effective role description is set out at http://teamcoachingtoolkit.com/roles-descriptions/

7. Agreement of the management of conflict

Most large projects begin in a spirit of optimism. Intellectually stimulated by the technical problems to be solved, the project participants come together with a sense that provided the structures and processes are in place, then everything will proceed smoothly. I have come across very few new teams who envisaged that they will come into conflict with each other at some stage later in the programme. And yet conflict is inevitable on a large project.

Technical arguments on the best way to approach a problem are something to be encouraged. Having different views and experiences around the table has been consistently shown to improve the quality of the outcome. Task-based conflict will not occur, however, unless people feel they can work in a psychologically safe environment. Invariably, conflict slows things down as everyone involved must either stop or go slow until a way forward is agreed. Most destructive of all is interpersonal conflict, where a dispute escalates, or possibly emanates from differences between individuals. Humans are meaning-making creatures who are continually seeking signals of threat to our own safety or the safety of our tribe. Consequently, it does not take a great deal of perceived provocation until we decide we are under threat and must defend ourselves. When interpersonal conflict occurs within a team it can be highly damaging as people take sides or simply disengage.

More often within a Big Team, you will find sub-teams who find a reason to come into conflict with each other, particularly where they have become aligned in vertical silos, and where horizontal interconnections are weak. We are going to look at conflict in more detail in Chapter 8. The lesson to be taken on board at the start-up phase is to answer the question 'what will we do when we come into conflict?'

8. Recognition of the need for iterative learning

It is a peculiar phenomenon, but I rarely come across a project team who include learning as a core part of their modus operandi. Perhaps I should not be surprised as most people who are selected to lead and deliver large projects are chosen on the basis that they know what they are doing. Once again, this is a reflection of orange-stage thinking where the underlying belief is that the future is largely predictable. The underlying belief is that if someone has worked on a similar large project before, they will know what to do on the next one.

In a complex environment, this cannot be true, as by definition, complex projects have too many changing variables to adopt a mechanistic approach. In the 21st century, every major project will have so many distinct facets that it will make it unique. Constructing a telecommunications network or a transport hub in one city will have many different elements to a similar project in another location, even though the underlying technology or construction process is identical. Every project has a new mix of people, politics and process, requiring a new team to quickly learn how to adapt how they work. Previous experience is nevertheless extremely useful, but value lies less in having experienced what happened before, and more in understanding how to apply previous learning to a new situation or environment.

Writing this book in 2019, it is becoming increasingly apparent that digital technologies are going to be increasing disruptive, offering opportunities and creating threats that project leaders have never previously encountered. Successful teams are therefore going to have to go through periods of accelerated learning as they gain experience in short experimental bursts of activity. The agile project management practices that have become common in the software industry are starting to find their way into other project environments.

Establishing a culture of learning is therefore going to be a prerequisite of any successful Big Team. The learning practices and habits the team is going to use must be included in the early thinking of any team. The key to learning within project teams is to focus on learning as a group, rather than individual development. The topic of accelerated learning is covered in more depth in Chapter 5.

Disseminating the core principles

As indicated above, once the ILT has worked through the above exercises, they should be able to articulate a set of core principles that will help inform the set-up workshops for each subsequent sub-team. I should emphasize again that this process is not intended to create a homogeneous collection of teams that are all required to think and behave according to the rules set down by the ILT. This is not only impractical but also unnecessary. Alignment is about getting each of the teams facing the same direction and collaborating based on a common understanding of the principles upon which the project is intended to work.

As discussed however, in a complex project environment, a cultural proposition cannot be imposed from above. It must be bought into by the sub-teams. Buy-in is therefore achieved by requiring each sub-team to go through a review of the same eight elements. The difference is that they should be asked to consider the outputs of the ILT sessions and ask themselves questions along the lines of:

- So, what does this mean to us?
- How would we apply those principles?
- Where would that principle create problems for us?
- What else do we want to add that will govern how we work?

It is inevitable, and to a certain extent desirable, that each team develops its own subculture within its own stories and values. Each team will have people who have different influences and even different cultural drivers. The value of using a consistent framework for team set-up is that in all probability having decided that the initial principles will work, the subculture will align to the cultures in the rest of the 'fleet'.

The point, however, is that the pioneering team cannot hope to create a set of teams that each follow the rules set by the leadership. Going back to the distinction between green and orange teams, in complex projects the leadership must expect each sub-team to evolve in the way that suits its members. The challenge with each of the set-up elements is to set out the high-level guidelines and then require each team to decide how they are going to implement them.

Co-creation

The underlying philosophy of team set-up is to encourage the collective agreement of the principles that will govern how the teams are going to work together both as individual units and also a collective team of teams. This requires the act of co-creation where those people who are going to meet, communicate and deliver their respective outputs first take the time to discuss, explore and then agree how they are going to work together. An explicit set of rules or standard procedures should emerge from this process that allows the team to become more effective even though this might require some of the team members to change their own preferred style or approach.

Humans have a peculiar view of rules, particularly in some Western societies. Whilst we find comfort and security in a degree of conformity, we tend to often baulk at rules or laws that may require us to do something we find inconvenient. We therefore frequently work around or even ignore certain rules that we regard as troublesome, particularly where we feel the rules have been imposed upon us. We are, however, much more likely to stick to the rules if we feel that we have played a role in their creation.

Co-creation allows a group to take ownership of their way of working so they become 'our rules' rather than 'their rules'. The process of co-creation therefore requires time to be set aside to talk, think, debate and agree. One cannot rush how others in a team think, although through the skilful use of questions one can influence their thinking process. The art of co-creation is to find the right physical environment and then facilitate the series of discussions using a workshop format that will shape how the team is going to behave when they meet together, and when they are working apart.

One of the underlying themes of this book is to recognize that success in Big Teams is less about the process of driving sequential activity and more about adapting plans quickly in response to changes in the external environment. The exercises I am advocating as part of the set-up process should not be treated as a schedule of activity that is conducted because someone outside of the team thinks it is a good idea. The exercises work when they stimulate thought and discussion, so make time to do them thoroughly.

Summary

This chapter has shown you what needs to be done to set a team up so that it is aligned to the cultural and behavioural norms that are needed to cope with the challenges posed by major projects. None of these activities is difficult or complicated, but each requires a degree of skill to create the desired outcome. The ILT and each subsequent sub-team need to commit time as part of the mobilization programme to work through each of the elements. The pressure to move quickly into technical delivery will be strong, but should be resisted. Virtually every study on team effectiveness highlights the need for teams to go through some form of positive socialization process that sets the rules on how they will work together. In a Big Team, this process must extend beyond the internal dynamics of the individual sub-teams to include a broader perspective on the interpersonal connections and relationships between teams.

One way or another, a team's behaviours are established at the start. As a leader, your ability to influence a team's behaviour is strongest in the first few weeks of a team's formal existence. After that, behavioural norms start to become more embedded and can be difficult to change. Time invested in getting your team into alignment is going to save a lot of time and effort later on.

Having managed to get your teams aligned, however, does not mean they will stay that way. Going back to the 'fleet' analogy, once you begin the voyage, the boats will be continuously changing direction. The next set of challenges within a Big Team is to put in place the activities and processes that will keep them broadly following the same route towards the destination. This is the subject of Chapter 6, but before we move onto that there is a critically important element that leaders of a Big Team need to take some time to consider. To build performance, each team must consider how they are going to learn for *the benefit of the project*. This is the subject of the next chapter.

Chapter 5
Accelerated learning

Embarking on a major project in the 21st century imposes a new type of pressure on a team of teams: the need to learn quickly as the project advances. Modern projects rarely sit within a single technical discipline such as engineering or construction. Tomorrow's projects will increasingly require specialists from a wide range of disciplines to come together as cross-functional teams to solve problems that have never previously been considered. The huge advances in digital technology over the last decade mean that every industry, business sector and profession must react to the opportunities and competitor threats thrown up by advances in data capture and analysis, robotics and artificial intelligence. Even conservative industries such as construction, which are typically very slow to adopt new ideas, are having to think hard about how new digital technology will fit within their service or product offer.

A large complex project will throw up problems and questions that the people involved will not have encountered before. Answering the questions and finding the solutions require a collection of minds working together, taking on new information and exploring ideas and options. This is a process of collective rather than individual learning, which is then used for the benefit of the project. The capability of a team to learn will govern its ability to deliver. Team learning activity should therefore be treated as a performance metric. This chapter looks at the concept of learning within teams and the barriers that get in the way of learning. I also offer some thoughts on how to create the right environment in which the teams can work as units to acquire and then apply newly acquired knowledge.

Team learning vs individual learning

In the first chapter we talked about how the difficulties created by the increased scale of modern projects add a level of complexity to major projects that few project leaders have previously been exposed to. If you then factor in the problems that arise from novelty, you can see that for most of the participants any major project is going to be a significant learning experience. Given that large projects tend to attract a wide range of competent and knowledgeable people, it is therefore surprising that most project environments are actually very poor at stimulating learning that can be used *for the benefit of the project*.

I have often encountered projects where many of the senior individuals join with the mindset that they have all of the required skills and knowledge to do the job they signed up to do, and that there is little need to make any further investment in new learning. They consequently resist initiatives that require time be spent in reflection and discussion on anything that is not directly related to the task in hand. I believe that part of the problem is cultural, in that too many adults equate learning with training. The educational process in most countries is based around systems for passing on specified blocks of information. Secondary, tertiary and even professional education is focused on the accumulation of qualifications. In the organizational environment, the prevailing theory is that new skills are best developed by having employees attend training courses, where each person is exposed to the same information in the hope that such exposure will result in the delegates learning how to perform in a different way.

The result is that people disconnect the concept of learning for their own benefit from the idea that learning is needed to also benefit an organization or project. Learning is seen as a matter of personal development rather than an exercise in business improvement. Consequently, few organizations and even fewer project teams make an allowance, either in time or in systems, for teams to collectively pause, reflect and agree alternative approaches that might improve effectiveness of the team's work.

It is therefore useful to separate the concept of individual learning from the knowledge accumulated by, and generated from, a team. Individual learning is obviously personal. As individuals we are learning all the time where each experience is stored in our minds and used to help us make decisions in the future. Team learning is different. Whether or not collective experience is of future value depends upon the extent to which the people in the team are able to articulate a common understanding of what has happened and what it means to them as a team.

What we learn as a team is about what is collectively, as opposed to individually, valuable. This is a natural process for all groups. At a most basic level, the collective question being asked is 'what are we doing that is moving us towards our goal and what is getting in the way?' Most teams can work out what does and doesn't work through trial and error. However, the pace demanded in most modern projects allows limited time for incremental experimentation. Teams working in complex environments need to find out what works and then adapt quickly.

LESSONS NOT LEARNED

My observation from the many projects I have either been a part of, or have researched, is that team learning is rarely a feature considered important to successful delivery. This is illustrated by the concept of lessons learned: a process widely understood to be an exercise carried out at the end of a project so that the knowledge and experiences gained can be passed on to the next project. I have nothing against the lessons learned concept in principle but in reality few organizations make systematic use of the process to actually improve productivity and effectiveness.

The lesson learned mechanism is typically regarded by project managers as an activity that takes place *after* the completion of the project. In theory, the project participants come together to reflect on what has happened and what learning should be recorded and passed on. Nice idea, but for a number of reasons it hardly ever takes place. Typical excuses include:

- lack of interest by the client/sponsor;
- lack of interest by key participants;
- no budget to cover costs;
- participants are too busy on new projects; and
- too long a time gap between project start and completion.

On the few occasions I have seen a lessons learned session take place, the commissioning organization then had no established system as to how to store or disseminate the output. The learning was therefore lost when the project team moved on.

Blockers to team learning

A key performance objective should be to embed team learning not just as a process but as a distinct part of the team's culture. This may be more challenging than is immediately apparent. You will need to avoid, or remove, the following blockers to team learning:

Complacency

One of the most insidious blockers to team learning is a belief within the team that time spent in review and reflection is unnecessary. Teams that adopt an underlying narrative that 'we have done this before and we know what we are doing' are unlikely to prioritize time to pause regularly and take stock of their progress until it is too late. Complacent teams also tend to shift quickly into blame mode when things go wrong as their self-belief tends to eliminate the possibility that they may have contributed to their own misfortune.

Not invented here

An extension of complacency is the rejection by a team of ideas or experiences from outside the team. This often stems from a degree of arrogance in the more senior members of the team, who have been very successful in the past and who see themselves a somehow elite and better than others. They consequently quickly reject ideas and experiences from outside. Rather than adapting new concepts to their circumstances, alternative approaches are rejected solely because they come from a different sector/industry or even another team on the project.

No time to learn

The most common of all the potential blockers to learning is the perennial excuse that there is not enough time, as the project is driven by unrelenting deadlines. I have only a limited amount of sympathy with this viewpoint as it tends to reflect an underlying belief that team learning is an optional extra rather than a critical element of team performance. In complex projects all teams will encounter new problems and will inevitably find they must spend unplanned time resolving them. Teams unwilling to take time to learn frequently end up in a downward spiral where they are continually trying to catch up with the programme, but fail to find ways to improve that would end up saving time in the future.

Groupthink

Another collective phenomenon that limits a team's ability to learn is a tendency towards a tacit or unspoken agreement amongst a team to only see one possible perspective to a problem. Groupthink tends to occur in homogeneous teams where the team members come from similar personal or professional backgrounds or in teams where a culture of consensus is very important. The problem with collective viewpoints is that whilst teams quickly come to an agreement over a proposed course of action, they become quickly closed to the possibility of alternative solutions.

Organizational politics

It is very difficult to establish a team learning culture in a highly politicized environment where individuals are more focused on jostling for position or influence. When people are concerned about their own advancement then the ability to share thoughts, ideas and feelings is very limited.

Conflicting environments

Linked to the above is the blockage to team learning created by conflict, either within a team or even between a team and an external party. Conflict generates emotions that affect how people feel. Perspectives tend to be limited and positions become entrenched. It is very difficult to take on new ideas and thinking in such an environment.

Functional stupidity

There is another blocker to learning that deserves a mention, known as 'functional stupidity'. Mats Alvesson and Andre Spicer, authors of *The Stupidity Paradox* (2016), describe functional stupidity as the inclination to reduce the scope of one's thinking and focus only on the narrow technical aspects of the job. The primary observation can be summarized in the following quote (2016, p. 9):

> When people are seized by functional stupidity they remain capable of doing the job, but they stop asking searching questions about their work. In the place of rigorous reflection, they become obsessed with superficial appearances. Instead of asking questions they start to obey commands. Rather than thinking about outcomes they focus on the techniques for getting things done.

Their point is that the institutionalization of many organizations and firms means they have built a culture that is unable to accommodate smart thinking to the point that they have developed mechanisms that actively discourage any serious discussion of alternative ideas. The effect of functional stupidity is that intelligent and capable people often cease to engage their minds fully when at work, and fall into routine. Functional stupidity should not theoretically ever feature in a project environment, as there are too many issues and problems that require intelligent consideration. However, on very large projects, one can often find individuals seconded from organizations in which the need to think and learn is deemed unnecessary. If such individuals are given a position of influence or authority, team learning is likely to be limited.

The simple message is that leaders must firstly consider to what extent they are potentially likely to create these blockers themselves and, having understood the implications, take the necessary steps to ensure the way is clear for the team to develop a learning culture.

Learning humility

Major projects tend to recruit and attract experienced professionals who typically join the team with not only extensive technical knowledge but also a number of preconceptions as to how the project will work. If your mind is closed to new ideas and concepts then you are unlikely to learn very quickly. I have been continually reinforcing the point that a large project is complex because there are so many new technical, commercial and social interfaces to be understood and managed. Humility is therefore required by all members of the team to acknowledge they cannot possibly have all the answers at the start and must be open to learning together to find the best way forward.

I recently came across a very technically competent team who felt they were leaders in their field. They were continually finding themselves in conflict with the client's team and were struggling to move on from the early design stage. Having gone through a number of exhausting rounds of negotiation, they finally found a way through. One of the senior directors explained that they had previously managed to get themselves into a place where they were so certain of their own position, they disregarded any thought of the client's perspective. Once they came to recognize the need to understand the client and their sponsors, they were able to find common ground and move forward.

This might seem like normal good negotiation practice but the real lesson for this particular group was the need to recognize they did not have all of the answers and so were able to shift their mental filters to be open to different perspectives and ideas. As the team moved into the next stage, they were able to accelerate the adoption of ideas and processes that were completely new both to them and the client team, helping them draw back time in the programme that had been lost during the period of conflict.

This story illustrates an interesting feature of many of successful teams I have encountered. They were all able to identify a point in the programme when 'things just seemed to click', and activity and task progression start to accelerate. The lift-off point always took some time to arrive, and often followed a short period of crisis that provided the catalyst for change. In each case, however, the team had spent time going through some of the learning processes described below, and had started to recognize both their individual limitations, and their collective potential.

This phenomenon is illustrated in Figure 5.1, which reintroduces the team performance curve from Chapter 1 (Figure 1.2). In the early mobilization stages, output is limited as individuals work out the challenges ahead. As team go through the learning process, and begin to understand and trust each other, their effectiveness increases. This observation is supported by Katzenbach and Smith (1993) who identified a similar performance curve for operational teams, where output actually drops initially before later accelerating. Their research confirms the inescapable reality that teams working on large projects cannot jump into a high-performing mode from day one. Each sub-team must learn to become an effective unit within itself, and then learn to become a connected unit within a Big Team. Teams that do not invest in team learning face a more common reality as illustrated by the dotted line, which shows that despite a certain amount of progression, performance eventually stagnates.

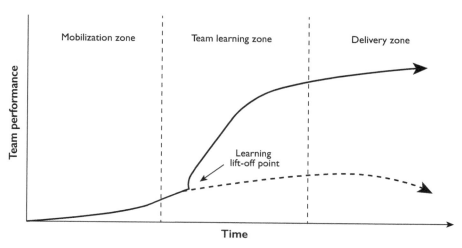

Figure 5.1 Team performance curve showing lift-off point

Psychological safety

The key to effective team learning is to create an environment where every person around the table feels sufficiently comfortable to be able to express their thoughts without fear of ridicule or retribution. In other words, they feel psychologically safe. The basepoint for research into this concept is Amy Edmondson's (1999) paper entitled 'Psychological safety and learning behaviour in work teams'. Her paper, based on a study of 51 work teams in a manufacturing company, concluded that psychological safety was directly linked to a team's ability to learn, and, consequently, its ability to perform effectively.

She defines psychological safety in the context of a team as being 'a shared belief that the team is safe for interpersonal risk taking'. This belief is usually tacit, or unexpressed, and as such is taken for granted by the team members. Edmondson makes the point that psychological safety is not the same as group cohesiveness, in that the need to maintain cohesion may often mean the members do not disagree or challenge. The term is not meant to imply an open disregard for group norms, but instead is a sense of confidence within the team that no one is going to be humiliated or punished if they speak up.

As Google's findings in Project Aristotle (https://rework.withgoogle.com) revealed, establishing psychological safety in a team is one of the primary conditions for raising team performance. There is a compulsive logic that if people working on projects need to be good at creative problem-solving, then the more often leaders can create a psychologically safe climate, the greater the chances of achieving a successful outcome. One therefore has to ask the question as to why psychological safety is an issue. After all, project professionals are usually polite and well behaved, so surely most teams operate as safe environments? This is an incorrect assumption. Most people can think of a group or team dominated by one or two individuals and where few others speak in meetings or offer up new ideas. Many organizational cultures tend to quickly fall into hierarchical team structures where the leader is expected to know what is happening and the remainder of the team operate in some form of unspoken pecking order, which sets rules on who speaks and what is discussed. In some organizations, particularly those with dysfunctional cultures, internal politics stimulate continual jockeying for position and influence. In such a climate, people will tend to display conscious and subconscious aggression in how they communicate. Over time, a pattern of behaviour forms where team members quickly learn to be very cautious in saying what they think.

It is easy to imagine psychologically unsafe meetings where dominant individuals belittle or ignore more submissive team mates. Psychological safety is a little more complicated as it is just as easy to create an unsafe environment in which team behaviours are observed as polite or neutral. The problem with humans is that we can find many reasons to be fearful, many of which can be quite personal. Dan Radecki and Leonie Hull (2018) explain that the brain is essentially a prediction machines that establishes patterns from our experiences, maps them and then hardwires them as blueprints for living to keep us safe. So our minds are continually scanning for signals that might indicate danger. In the modern workplace, we are unlikely to be physically attacked but we nevertheless retain a negativity bias, where our defence systems are tuned at a subconscious level to treat anything other than positive nonthreatening signals as being a cause for alarm. Our alarm system may then drive inappropriate reactions and behaviours.

If we were to allow these ancient defence mechanisms to dominate our lives, we would be unable to function effectively in the modern world. Fortunately, as Radecki and Hull point out, we have a co-pilot in the brain known as the prefrontal cortex, which is able to engage in conscious and logical thinking processes. This part of the brain allows us to manage our emotional reactions, even if it cannot control them. This is where emotional intelligence becomes a key leadership skill, in that the way to help others around the table feel safe enough to speak is to send out positive signals that will show they are not likely to be hurt.

Part of the set-up process is to train leaders in the skills that help establish psychological safety. As an illustration, such training would include developing capability in the following areas:

- Asking 'humble' questions – questions that are clearly phrased to show you do not know the answer and are seeking help.
- Active listening – how to look at the person who is giving a response and let them know they have your full attention.
- Demonstrating your understanding by validating comments.
- Demonstrating vulnerability – sharing your own past mistakes and owning up to gaps in your own knowledge to show it is acceptable not to have all of the answers.
- Using facial signals and open body language.
- Pacing meetings to slow down where necessary to encourage others to have the space to talk and to think.

Learning environment

Team learning is concerned with the collective acquisition of knowledge through shared experience. It is not therefore the role of the team leader to tell the rest of the team what they should know. Instead the team leader must own the responsibility for creating the environment or climate most conducive to team learning. This is less about the physical space in which a learning session should take place and more about the atmosphere in which the team can be encouraged to think. David Clutterbuck (2007) makes the point that effective learning environments require an emphasis on the willingness of the team to learn and to help others to learn. A positive learning environment is one where

- everyone's thoughts and ideas are valued;
- everyone has a right and a responsibility to question what they do not understand;
- mistakes are an opportunity to learn, not a reason to blame;
- asking others about how they feel or what they think is encouraged; and
- admitting ignorance is seen as a strength rather than a weakness.

Clutterbuck comments that when a team are satisfied that the above elements are in place, they are more likely not only to feel more comfortable with exploration of new ideas, but also to confront poor team behaviours and work processes. They are also likely to be more open to taking learning from outside the team. The main benefit, however, is that they are far more likely to apply the learning as a collective group.

The above list provides a relatively straightforward set of ground rules the team should agree to at the start of any review session. Actually sticking to them nevertheless takes practice, and the team leader, or whoever is facilitating the review session, must help the team learn to work out how they make these principles work in practice.

Team learning maturity

I mentioned that the ability of a team to learn should be seen as a performance issue. Learning should therefore be regarded as an essential element of a team's process, which is planned, executed and measured for its effectiveness. There is a maturity journey that each sub-team must go through to become effective in how they use learning for the benefit of the project. It begins with an awareness of fellow team members, and then about the connections with other sub-teams. The next step is to find the rhythms or cycles in which different types of learning can take place, and the steps to move through to build understanding and plan alternative approaches.

Intra- and inter-team awareness

The team must first work though the processes that will enable the team to learn about itself. This is part of the set-up process described in the previous chapter where the exercises help members become clear on their common purpose and can devote time to begin to understand each other. Using facilitating tools such as psychometric testing, team members can quickly learn about each other's drivers and preferences. Using storytelling exercises, they can learn about each other's past experiences and anything else they can bring to the project in addition to their technical specialism. These processes build trust within the team and help establish psychological safety, and are part of the early-stage alignment process.

The next element of team learning within a Big Team is to learn about other teams within the project with which there is a degree of overlap or interdependence. If you are going to be dependent on another team's performance to be able to deliver your part of a programme or workstream, it makes sense to understand as much as you can about their capability and capacity. Another part of the team learning journey is to take a methodical approach to exchanging information between teams that helps them understand more about each other. This is an important component of the team-of-teams concept, where inter-team connections move beyond a reliance on the one-to-one relationship between team leaders. Having a clear sense of the distinct cultural drivers that exist in each sub-team builds comprehension. The greatest value of inter-team understanding comes when teams know enough about each other to be able to provide support under pressure, and to quickly solve problems using a wider knowledge base.

As an illustration, one of my recent projects involved management of the interfaces arising between the client team and a number of primary contractors and suppliers. The wider project team had made the transition from design into delivery and was scaling up quickly. There were a lot of new people in leadership positions, and the client had learned the necessity of establishing good communications between sub-teams during the previous phase of project. A programme was put in place built around a framework that specifically required the following activities to be worked through between teams:

- finding clarity of understanding of each other's short- and long-term goals and objectives;
- testing what assumptions were being made about each other;
- agreeing rules of engagement for connection and communication between the teams;
- understanding each other's primary roles and accountabilities;
- agreeing a process for horizon scanning for future problems;
- agreeing to collect feedback on the success of the interface on a regular basis; and
- agreeing a protocol for early conflict resolution.

This ability to learn quickly about each other proved to be a vital factor in the success of the project. The process helped them build the types of personal Level Two relationships identified in the previous chapter and so, as the programme progressed, they were able to speed up decision making.

Short-cycle reviews

This is a learning mechanism that should take place very shortly after an element or iteration of a project has been completed. It is difficult to generalize just what constitutes an 'element' but I regard it as a component part of a stage. So, for example, it might be an intense period of activity that is likely to be repeated many more times over the project cycle. Short-cycle reviews or post-action reviews are short and practical. They should be performed quickly without the need for extensive deliberation unless, of course, the task was deemed a disaster, in which case a different type of learning structure is needed.

An example comes from a team working on an upgrade to a part of a railway network in the north of England. The team could only gain access to the track at weekends and had to fit in a lot of work over a 48-hour period before handing the site back to the rail operator. Whilst the particular tasks changed over time, the teams involved had become increasingly more efficient at planning and executing their work in the short time available to them. Every Tuesday morning the teams assembled to discuss the weekend's activity and agree what adjustments could be made to allow them to get more work done in the allotted period. Over a six-month period they were able to improve output by nearly 300% as they found better ways to organize resources and eliminate time wastage. The project manager who told me this story summarized the following lessons they learned in their post-action reviews:

- The reviews had to be done very quickly after the end of the work.
- As many of the team involved as possible should be present.
- It was really important to focus on improvement and not criticism.
- The agreed ideas must be written down into a short list and everyone present in the review should receive a copy.

The focus of discussion in a short-cycle review is on the actions that took place, examining what went well, what didn't and what could be changed. This process can be seen to apply to virtually any short-term activity undertaken by a team. The purpose is to share thinking about how to do a particular task, or series of tasks, more effectively.

End-of-stage reviews

An end-of-stage review goes deeper than a short-cycle review. A stage is a discrete section of the project where a series of activities has been completed and a new series is about to start. If a short cycle is roughly weekly then a stage typically takes place over a few months. The focus of attention in an end-of-stage review is looking back over the whole stage to consider what has happened across the programme, and how effectively the teams have worked together. This is partly a leadership team activity, but should also apply to the sub-teams since they are the ones most likely to identify problems and take remedial action. This part of the review cycle should look at what is happening in the wider team, rather than sub-team productivity.

An end-of-stage review is a strategic exercise where the team must take time to get a collective understanding of what they have been through and decide how their experiences inform their approach to the next stage. Some teams may see this as a lessons learned exercise, and, taken literally, that is what it is. My only caution in attaching this label is that I have found lessons learned sessions often have a tactical focus. They consequently often fail to seek the insights that come from taking deeper systemic perspective. An end-of-stage review should involve small groups of no more than seven or eight people so that everyone contributes. If possible, the review should also involve people from different disciplines to gain a wider perspective.

The learning here is less about efficiency of process and more about the effectiveness of the system. Peter Senge (1990) describes systems thinking as a discipline for seeing *wholes* rather than *parts*, for seeing *patterns of change* rather than *static snapshots* and for understanding the subtle interconnectedness that gives living systems their unique character. A paper issued by the Association of Project Management (2018, p. 6) adds a further useful explanation, observing that 'systems thinking acknowledges the relationship between interacting components. In doing this it helps to identify the leverage points where interventions will have the greatest impact, not just straight away, but over time.'

A discussion on the topic of systems thinking can quickly become very hypothetical and is therefore in danger of losing its value. When taken in the context of a major project, one might try to understand the 'system' as the visible and the invisible machinery that has been created by the project's participants so that it can achieve its objective. The visible parts are the prescribed processes and methodologies that try to ensure good governance and efficient management. The invisible element is the cultural and behavioural influences that impact on decision making and the manner in which the project plans are implemented. As you will have gathered by now, it is this invisible element that sits at the heart of most of the problems arising from complexity.

SYSTEMS THINKING

Complexity is a feature of a problem rather than the problem itself. In practical terms, complexity in projects arises because any major decision is likely to have an impact on a number of different interfaces both inside and outside the project. Consequently, decisions made to find a quick fix to issues tend to have side effects that were not anticipated and that may then make the problem worse.

Teams working in complex environments must therefore learn to think systemically, i.e. to understand the system that surrounds a particular problem. The concept of systemic thinking is a growing area of scientific study, which has the potential to provide some valuable insights when exploring large, difficult problems. The trouble is that much of the published work in this area is quite theoretical and it can be difficult to tie the concept back to resolving the challenges arising in Big Teams. The first step is to understand what is meant by a system. According to Donella Meadows (2009, p. 2) 'a system is a set of related components that work together in a particular environment to perform whatever functions are required to achieve the systems objective'.

The underlying principle of systems thinking is that everything is interconnected. In practical terms, this means that one cannot rely on a simplistic model of cause and effect where an action results in a single isolated outcome. Instead, a systemic perspective is concerned with causality, where one is looking for the deeper impacts an action, or series of actions, has through the system.

Another useful component of systems thinking is the idea of synthesis, where one is looking to combine two or more things to create a new whole. Synthesis can be seen as the opposite to analysis, which is focused on dissecting complexity into manageable parts. Since the parts of a complex system are dynamic rather than static, synthesis attempts to see the whole and the parts at the same time to understand the connectedness.

This links to a third element of systems thinking – the concept of emergence, which describes the outcome of when a number of system components interact that had not previously been anticipated.

Concepts such as causality, synthesis and emergence might initially appear to be too abstract to have any practical applications to the leadership and management of a Big Team. However, once you begin to see a Big Team as an interconnected network of sub-units interacting both within the project system and the wider environment, they become tools that help you look at the challenge of managing complex problems in a different way.

Learning pitfalls

A common point of reference when trying to understand how adults learn is the Kolb Learning Cycle (Kolb 1984), which identifies four stages moving from Action to Review to Reflect to Plan and then back to Action (Figure 5.2). This four-step model is useful in so far as it recognizes the different types of thinking required at each stage. The review process requires assembling the facts on what has happened whilst reflection is concerned with how the action has played out. The planning phase then requires anticipating the future and agreeing how the learning will be put into action.

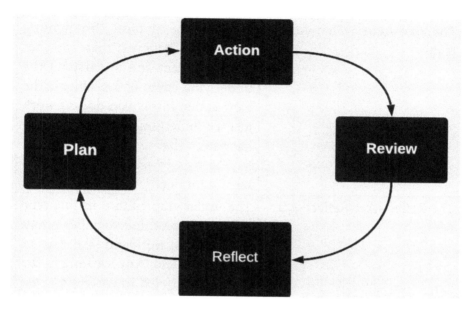

Figure 5.2 Kolb Learning Cycle (Kolb 1984)

A desire within a team to learn may not always lead to a new outcome or way of thinking. Peter Hawkins (2017) identifies a number of potential traps that teams can easily fall into, which will limit their ability to learn. The potential problem lies in the desire to take short cuts and miss out some of the stages, possibly driven by the different learning preferences of members of the team. Hawkins provides five examples of team habits that will limit learning, which are shown in Table 5.1.

My purpose in identifying these learning traps is to emphasize the point that learning as a team is not a simple matter of having a meeting to chat through what went wrong. To find understanding requires the team to work through a learning sequence in a structured manner. How this works in practice will depend upon the context of the team situation, but having this basic structure in mind should help.

Table 5.1 Team learning short cuts (adapted from Hawkins 2017)

Short cut sequence	*Team description*
The Plan-Action-Plan-Action team	This is the typical fire-fighting team that believes there is not time to reflect and understand the underlying cause of a problem. The view is that if the plan doesn't work just try something else and see what happens. The team will therefore have a bias towards tactical short-term thinking.
The Reflect-Act-Reflect-Act team	The underlying culture in this type of team is to think together about what did not work and take steps to fix the problem. Any learning in the team is restricted to correcting past errors but there is no focus on the future.
The Review-Reflect-Review-Reflect team	This is a team that likes to talk and explore ideas. Plans are developed but are never put into action. Such teams can be accused of creating 'talk shops' where the meetings are long and serious, but with no discernible output.
The Reflect-Plan-Reflect-Plan team	This team puts a lot of focus on thinking and planning but is hesitant to make decisions. This often reflects a lack of confidence and a desire to get more information before deciding to act. Such teams suffer from a 'paralysis by analysis'.

The Reflect-Act team	An authoritarian approach where the belief in the leadership team is that 'once we have thought about an issue, we will make a decision and instruct others to implement the actions'. This is a classic orange-stage style of leadership, which may be pragmatic but makes no allowance for feedback and is likely to create resistance in other parts of the team, reducing the opportunity for the learning to recycle back into the project.

Team learning sequence

Building upon the Kolb (1984) model, there is a sequence of activity that can be applied to teams working in a Big Team environment. Figure 5.3 sets out a model adapted from the work of David Cleden (2009) based on six primary steps.

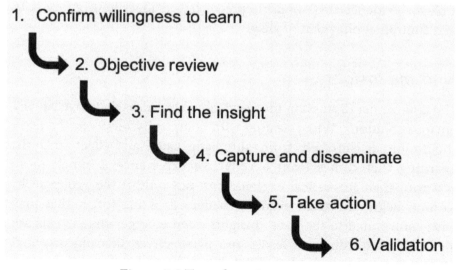

Figure 5.3 Team learning sequence

Confirm willingness to learn

It may seem an obvious point, but it would be a mistake to assume that a team is always ready to open their minds and seek to find new insights into how their role in the project might be improved. As discussed above, many large organizations degenerate into a state of functional stupidity, where thinking is regarded as less valuable than being seen to be supporting the status quo. A conversation needs to be had that draws the team away from 'going through the motions' of learning and towards a recognition of the benefits of acquiring new knowledge as a team.

Objective review

The next step is to review the issue under discussion. When looking back at a recent period of activity, if a lesson is to be learned then there needs to be a common understanding of what really happened. Cleden points out that it is impossible to be completely objective particularly when an activity has not gone to plan. The team must nevertheless recognize any tendency towards perceptual positions in which we only look for evidence that supports preconceived ideas and ignore data that contradict our point of view.

Find the insight

The issue under discussion may have obvious causes that have equally obvious solutions. When dealing with complexity however, the team should be discouraged from simplistic cause-and-effect analysis. Learning that comes from a collective experience is much more powerful than theoretical explanations, but only if the group seeks to look below the surface and consider all of the forces that may have contributed to the issue. Insights often emerge when events are viewed through different lenses and perspectives, offering potential explanations that are not immediately apparent.

Capture and disseminate

It surprises me how often a learning session closes in high spirts and a sense of achievement, but with few actions agreed as to how the new learning is to be recorded, disseminated or stored. These actions are perhaps the tedious element of the process, but if the new learning has not been recorded it cannot be recycled back into the project with any impact. Responsibility for capture and dissemination should be agreed at the start of the session and should be completed with an agreed time period, ideally less than five working days.

Take action

It should go without saying that unless the new learning is applied then the exercise has been a waste of time. Do not underestimate the challenge, however, of convincing other parts of the team to actually perform tasks in a different way. I was told of a major project that had encountered technical problems in a power scheme that had run severely over programme. A review session had been held, and an alternative approach agreed. The project leader was therefore quite agitated to find exactly the same problem occurring again six months later in a different part of the scheme. When asked for an explanation, he was given the excuse that the team involved decided that the action only affected the earlier phase and would not apply to the current part of the project!

Validation

The final element of Cleden's model points the team towards checking that the agreed actions have worked satisfactorily. As he comments, not all lessons deliver the expected benefits. If the new way of working was not useful then the problem may need to be revisited. Alternatively, if it worked well then it should be reinforced and publicized for consideration by other teams.

Summary

The point I have been trying to embed in this chapter is that learning is a vital factor in the ultimate success on a large project. Teams that aspire to high performance but that are unwilling to spend time exploring, theorizing and reflecting together are unlikely to achieve their potential. Most importantly, the new learning needs to be fed back into the project team, so further time needs to be invested to store and disseminate valuable new knowledge.

This component of the Big Team performance model stitches together the elements of alignment and engagement. Collective learning must build upon trust and mutual comprehension within and between teams, but it is also an effective mechanism making connections and improving relationships. Every team must work out its own approach, but for those who have the foresight to recognize the power of team learning, the downstream benefits are potentially huge.

Chapter 6
Maintain engagement

The project is now starting to build momentum, and more people are joining the wider team. Assuming you have taken on board the advice in Chapter 4 and have established a common framework for team set-up, then as new sub-teams are formed, they will have developed a common set of primary goals, and will understand the cultural parameters and behaviours required to work on the project. The sub-teams should therefore be aligned, each pointing broadly in the same direction. The challenge the project leadership now faces is to maintain that alignment as the teams move from the calm of the mobilization and planning phase into the more turbulent waters of delivery. The task is therefore to build engagement.

Engagement is a word that can have a number of meanings, but in the context of a major project it can be defined as a state in which people and teams are completely absorbed in their particular role, and are committed to the success of the enterprise. Engagement therefore sits largely in the minds of the project participants. Leaders cannot force their followers to be engaged. All they can do is to create the environment and hope the team will find their own drive and motivation. It is this human variable that is often missing from the manuals and textbooks that set out the technical processes attached to project management. Amber- and orange-stage mindsets make a presumption that if a person or team is employed to work on a project they will automatically be engaged in their work. After all, this is what they are paid to do. Whether or not they find the tasks interesting, and enjoy working with their colleagues, is not a concern of the management team. This is, of course, a flawed assumption. Most experienced managers recognize that a task that on average takes 4 hours can often be completed in 2 hours by someone who is focused and motivated. Conversely, the same task might take 8 hours or longer by an individual who is disinterested.

As discussed in earlier chapters, getting a Big Team into alignment requires investment in terms of time and energy. This investment will, however, be wasted if alignment is not maintained. Without continued attention to the factors that influence team dynamics, leaders will find that much of their time is continually focused on resolving the problems created by people falling back into disruptive patterns of behaviour. This chapter considers some of the challenges Big Teams face in trying to build and maintain commitment, and the particular obstacles that must be overcome to create a culture of collaboration.

The slippery slope of team engagement

A project environment can be thought of as an upward slope. It starts on a gentle gradient, but becomes much steeper as the project moves into the execution phases. Moving uphill requires energy, and as we tire we are more likely to revert to selfish, less collaborative behaviours. People start to fall into the traps that are created by trying to take short cuts based on short-term transactional thinking. These forces can be thought of as behavioural gravity. In the mobilization or set-up phase the gradient is slight and so the teams have the time and energy to focus on building positive collaborative habits. This can be thought of as the conditioning phase where the team get themselves fit to cope with the exertions ahead. As the project moves forward, the gradient steepens as they are tested by the pressure of workload.

Those teams who are 'fit' enough to keep moving uphill eventually find they have embedded the habits and practices of effective teamwork. The pull of behavioural gravity therefore lessens as they build trust and develop stronger relationships. The team environment has, however, a slippery surface and so it can be easy to slide backwards when under pressure. The role of the leadership is to recognize those forces that impact on team behaviours as they move into delivery, and wherever possible seek to reduce the gradient of the slope.

Team motivation

Project performance is directly connected to the motivation and drive of the individuals within the sub-teams. The greater the level of engagement, the more likely they will remain motivated. We are motivated by our own particular drivers, some of which are inherited, some learned and some as a reaction to our immediate circumstances. Motivation cannot be imposed, but it can be heavily influenced by the actions of others. Motivation can be separated into two elements: *extensive* and *intrinsic*. Extrinsic motivation is driven by external reward, typically financial, but might also include the receipt of goods or services people need to get by in our day-to-day lives. However, extrinsic factors tend to work at a superficial level, and generally once we have all of the basic elements of food, warmth and physical security, adding higher amounts of external reward does not necessarily increase individual motivation.

Much more powerful is the drive that comes from intrinsic motivators. These arise from within a person in that they satisfy a need or desire to achieve something or behave in a particular way. Dan Pink (2009) identifies three distinct elements of intrinsic motivation:

1. Autonomy – The ability to direct our own lives and work so that we feel we can control what we do, when we do it and with whom we work.
2. Mastery – A desire to improve a skill or capability through learning and practice, often just for personal satisfaction.
3. Purpose – A sense of doing something for a higher purpose either as a contribution to society at large or for a particular group that needs help.

Recognizing these intrinsic motivators can be useful when considering how to build and maintain engagement. Overtime payments for working at weekends and bonus payments on achieving certain deadlines can often be a useful mechanism to encourage additional effort in particular circumstances. Many managers find, however, that, over time, extrinsic rewards have a diminishing impact as people become less interested in additional income versus leisure time. Alternatively, team members become used to working more hours, but spread their workload to fill a longer day with little additional output.

Building intrinsic motivation requires enabling sub-teams where possible to have a say in how they work, encouraging a pursuit of excellence and finding ways to find a sense of contribution to something of wider value. Some projects may achieve this directly where the project has some direct social benefit, for example building a specialist medical centre. I have seen other more commercial projects where time and resources were set aside to support local charitable initiatives. The point to emphasize here is that increased productivity is as likely to come from enabling the teams to feel they are part of something bigger than themselves. Money is important but only takes collective motivation so far. To encourage teams to input additional discretionary effort takes some thought.

Discretionary effort

Discretionary effort sits at the heart of high performance. This is usually seen in team members who choose to work additional time, reflecting a desire and a commitment to complete tasks to a high standard or to meet challenging deadlines. The point, however, is that each individual must feel they make the choice to do additional work, rather than feel there is an obligation placed on the entire team. Being coerced to work additional hours will rarely produce much additional output, as people who feel imposed upon will fill the working day with non-productive activities instead. When we recognize we have a choice, however, our intrinsic drivers are allowed to come to the surface.

Intrinsic motivation is often the force that drives sub-team performance as individuals seek to help each other when the team is collectively under pressure. When the project environment creates the right level of stimulus, if a part of the team decide to step up their level of commitment the rest will often follow.

Discretionary effort cannot be taken for granted and should not be presumed. I once worked with a small firm of specialist consultants who wrote specifications for architects and engineers. They had a culture of never missing a deadline and were very proud of their reputation. The managers rarely asked their staff to work overtime, but the collective mindset was that, in busy periods, the working week was often extended into longer days and weekends as needed. The firm was acquired by a multinational engineering consultancy, whose standard contract was 40 hours a week, whilst the contracted hours for the specification writers were only 37.5 hours a week. Since the specialist team were usually working in excess of 45 hours a week, the new management assumed that no one would object if they aligned the contracts of their new acquisition with everyone else in the firm. This turned out to be a huge mistake. The effect was an immediate work-to-rule as the specification writers now felt the organization was taking advantage of their commitment. Performance suffered and within six months many of the team had left the business.

The silo effect

Large groups of people working within a Big Team need to be organized into some form of structure. Most large projects begin at a small scale, which is able to function around a loose management and communication framework. However, as the team grows in size, sub-groups will naturally form as people clump together around some form of common activity. As projects scale from 5 to 50 to 500 to 5,000 people, there needs to be some order and consistency in how people are recruited, managed, paid, and so on.

The traditional organization chart has evolved as a two-dimensional structure with horizontal and vertical lines whose connections indicate who is in which 'gang'. Earlier in the book, I made the observation that the delivery of tasks in a major project relies on a loose framework of connections that are better understood as a three-dimensional network rather than a two-dimensional 'org chart'. However, humans like the sense of stability that comes with the traditional two-dimensional structure. We tend to want to know who is the person who is authorized to decide what we do, who will take care of us, as well as who is taking care of them. Reporting lines allow us to make sense of the day-to-day functioning of an organization, even if they don't provide an accurate representation of how the project actually works.

The traditional 'org chart' is not likely to disappear in the near future and projects will continue to be organized around structures with more vertical lines than horizontal ones. Seen in two dimensions, projects need to be organized in such a manner as to provide the most effective way of delivering the outcome. This is not, however, always obvious. Should teams be assembled according to task, geographic location, technical specialization or some other form of grouping? Whatever classification is chosen will inevitably lead to the creation of groups working within distinct boundaries, which over time form into 'silos'.

In organizational terms, a silo is a group or department that operates to a greater or lesser extent in isolation from other parts of the same organization. The key word here is isolation, implying that the group works alone, having limited contact with others in the organization. One of the themes of this book is for sub-teams to work collaboratively with each other, which would imply a need to set up a project to avoid silos. The requirement for organization, however, means that distinct groups will inevitably form in line with whichever arrangement is chosen to measure and manage team activity. The leadership's task is therefore not so much to prevent silos forming, but to diminish their ability to disrupt collaboration. It is therefore helpful to have an understanding of the forces that create silos.

Tribal tendencies

The need to belong to a familiar group or tribe is deeply rooted in human DNA. We tend to be most comfortable with our extended family, our friends and people who we perceive to be similar to ourselves. Given a choice, most people will tend to stay within groups with whom they are familiar and only interact with outsiders on a transactional basis.

Collaborating with others does not come naturally and, in fact, is a learned skill. In times of uncertainty or perceived threat we will revert to the security of our tribe. We also have a tendency to find reasons to come into conflict with adjacent tribes, as this helps reinforce our own sense of identity and belonging.

Even without the threat of conflict, humans in groups often become competitive. Muzafar Sherif (1966) used a study of boys in a summer camp to explore the issue of inter-group conflict. The boys were organized into groups that then competed against each other in a number of games and activities. Sherif observed that even though the selection of membership of the groups was quite arbitrary, the boys quickly formed negative beliefs about the other groups. His conclusion was that competition has a negative effect as conflict emerged between the groups even when they were not taking part in an event.

Daniel Levi (2017) points to social identity theory developed by Tajfel and Turner (1986) who postulate that a person's self-worth is linked to the groups to which he or she is attached, and consequently they see their own group as superior to others. When teams feel they are in competition, they tend to not only increase internal cohesion but also become isolated themselves from external influence.

In competitive situations the focus of a team tends to be on the task in hand, and social and emotional issues tend to be ignored, to the long-term detriment of the team. Ironically it can be the winning teams that suffer as much as the losing teams. Forsyth and Kelly (1996) noted that winning teams will attribute success to their own superiority and consequently fail to take time to repair the behavioural problems that develop in all social groups over time. On the flip side, losing teams often succumb to an emotional urge to blame each other, rather than understand how to improve.

There are, however, times when a bit of friendly competition between teams can be useful to improve performance. There will often be phases on large projects where scale requires multiple sub-teams to be assembled to complete similar tasks. When reviewing progress there will inevitably be comparisons between teams based on whatever data are used to monitor how each team is performing. I have found that creating league tables on particular metrics can have a dramatic effect on team behaviour. Few teams like to be seen as sitting at the bottom of the league table and, to the extent that they are able, will quickly begin to focus on those activities that affect the metrics. Using competition between sub-teams can be a valuable mechanism for improving productivity and implementing change initiatives.

Fiefdoms

Tribal instincts become particularly problematic when the team leader tries to shape their team into a distinct 'fiefdom'. In medieval times, a fiefdom was an area of territory granted to a favoured individual that, provided he continued to show allegiance to his benefactor, he could run as he wished without oversight. In the modern world, a fiefdom is a section or division of a project run by an individual who wishes to control his/her own part of the project. In project fiefdoms, the leader often tries to separate the people under his/her authority from the rest of the wider team. The effect is to create a subculture in which his/her team feel they are different from others and do not need to conform to the practices and norms being adopted elsewhere in the project.

In the course of my research, I was given an example of a project where the work packages were split into three streams, each under the ownership of a senior project manager. One, let us call him John, had been in the industry for 20 years whereas his two counterparts were much less experienced. As the works progressed, problems began to emerge because the three project leaders did not appear to be communicating outside of the periodic progress meetings. Resources were being duplicated and a regular stream of issues was coming back to the project director as a result of poor coordination. Information sharing with the other teams was negligible, and so when problems occurred John was quick to blame the issues on the inadequacies of the other two leaders, who lacked the experience to push back. Repeated delays eventually forced the director to move John off the programme as it became clear that he was working to a policy of isolating his team from the other two groups.

Interestingly, John's team thought he was a great leader. They felt he looked after their interests and had created a strong team culture. Delving deeper into the story, it was interesting to note that John had built his career doing projects his own way. He was good at leading a team of a size where he was able to manage all of the key interactions and be the primary decision maker. He was therefore very successful in delivering projects up to a certain size. Stepping up to a much larger programme of works was difficult for him as he had never had to learn the skills needed for genuine collaboration over the period of a programme. His instinct was therefore to try to ring-fence his part of the project and then revert to the mechanisms and practices that had worked for him in the past.

Silos are an inevitable consequence of the need to organize large teams into manageable structures. At the start of a project, the barriers that separate internal teams are relatively thin, as numbers are small and everyone knows each other. The task of management is to ensure the inevitable barriers that form between teams do not thicken over time, whilst also maintaining initiatives that encourage cross-silo communication and collaboration.

Establishing a collaborative environment

Throughout the book I have stressed the need for Big Teams to be set up so that different sub-teams work together to solve problems and find creative alternatives to deliver the desired outcomes. This can only be achieved by working in collaboration. Collaboration is a somewhat vague concept in that it is commonly defined as 'a situation where two or more people work together to create or achieve the same thing'. Collaboration could be seen as an activity in itself, but it makes more sense to view it as an outcome of other more specific activities such as sharing ideas and resources. The objective of the leadership team is to establish a collaborative environment, as a part of a collaborative culture, where it is understood to be 'normal' to provide assistance to other teams without demanding immediate reward. Unfortunately this is not a state that can be created on demand. A collaborative environment evolves over time, as individuals build personal (Level Two) relationships and begin to trust each other. Simply working together does not necessarily imply collaboration. The distinguishing feature is a willingness of the parties to provide discretionary effort to help each other, although not necessarily at the same time.

The drivers for collaboration can be personal, commercial or both. Personal drivers might derive from a passion to achieve the outcome, a strong personal relationship with the other party, or simply a belief that providing assistance is the right thing to do. Commercial drivers might arise from a mutual understanding that by providing assistance in the short term, the other party will return the favour at some unspecified point in the future.

Collaboration therefore relies on trust being created between the parties. As project leader you cannot force other people to trust each other, as this is a personal issue. You can, however, try to ensure that the obstacles to trust are removed or diminished. The systemic obstacles that can impede collaboration include:

- initiatives or activities where the parties perceive a degree of coercion to compete with each other, either for resources, future work or influence;
- a lack of common processes or platforms, which means the parties have to expend additional effort just to begin to work together;
- a lack of flexibility in structures and the programme that inhibits the team's ability to explore potential areas of collaboration;
- a need for control, where parties are discouraged from having discussions outside of the formal hierarchical communication channels;
- allowing the evolution of a fear-based culture, where seeking help is seen as a sign of weakness; and
- the imposition of short-term transactional arrangements where external suppliers are forced into contracts with very low margins and hence little capacity to provide services beyond their contracted scope.

Building a collaborative culture

For the reasons outlined above, people in a working environment do not therefore always find collaboration easy. The more important collaboration is to the project, the more effort needs to be applied by leadership to diminish the effect of the blockers and to promote a collaborative culture. I have set out a number of suggestions below.

Collaboration policy

Embedding collaboration as an element of the project's culture is a great example of an actionable value. Steps can be taken that will help shift the concept of collaboration into a series of practical actions that become integrated into the programme. It therefore becomes part of the planning process and has greater chance of being properly funded. I have come across many projects where collaboration is agreed as being desirable, but is then pushed to the periphery of day-to-day activity. The outcome is that any time spent promoting initiatives to improve collaborative working practices and behaviours is largely wasted.

Modelling collaborative behaviour

One of the fastest ways to destroy the potential benefits of strong cultural values is for the project leaders to display behaviours that indicate opposing values. Project leaders and team leaders must take great care not to fall back into transactional behaviours when under pressure. Team members will not really believe in collaborative values unless they see their leaders behaving in a different way, and so modelling positive behaviours is essential, not optional. I have worked on a major project that invested millions in trying to build collaborative practices through the many sub-teams, only to waste it by demonstrating aggressive transactional behaviours from the senior leadership team when the costs began to overrun.

Develop collaborative skills

Another mistake is to assume that people know how to collaborate in a work environment. We instinctively know how to cooperate, but working culture tends to emphasize the need to protect your own team or organization and to treat outsiders with a degree of suspicion. Collaboration requires a number of distinct skills that can be learned through training and practice. A case can therefore be made for setting up a training programme that will help sub-team leaders and others who must connect and collaborate with other teams to build the required skills. A typical collaboration skills course might include the following:

- recognizing the blockers to working collaboratively;
- finding a common goal and purpose;
- building strong relationships;
- cross-team awareness; and
- learning the art of questioning and listening.

There are many other possible learning elements that could be added to the list, but to have the required impact the training course should be bespoke to the project. Where possible, it should sponsored and preferably co-led by a member of the leadership team.

Provide collaboration space

It is a very practical point, but people need space to exchange ideas and explore possible opportunities. Having the physical space that is easily accessible with the facility to draw on walls or flipcharts is an important asset for any project team. Too many meeting rooms are designed for people to talk, but exploring ideas and concepts needs more space. One of the most successful Big Teams I have recently encountered made specific provision for collaboration space when they set up the project office. A series of different sized rooms had floor to ceiling white boards, plus flipcharts and interactive screens. There were a few chairs and a small table, but the intention was that that more time would be spent standing rather than sitting. It was interesting to hear that the teams quickly became used to seeing this space as being a positive environment, where the atmosphere was more creative and solution-focused than in the other more formal meeting spaces.

Measure collaboration as a performance metric

If 'what gets measured gets done', then collaborative activity should be monitored as part of the project controls function. Collaborative activity is going to vary considerably from project to project and so there is no standard list of collaborative measurements. It therefore requires a degree of imagination and experimentation to work out what to monitor on your project. As an initial guide, consider the following questions:

- What would great collaboration look like at this stage of the project?
- What are the hard measures of activity we could record?
- What are the perceptual measures we could collect via feedback and what system would we use?
- What outcomes could we identify and monitor that could only come from or be enhanced by collaboration between the teams?

Tell the stories

Cultures build around stories of what works and what doesn't work for a group. Collaboration might need to work at an organizational level between two or more partners or it might occur between two engineers from different sub-teams trying to solve an unusual problem. When you find good examples of collaboration, communicate the stories to the rest of the wider team. Similarly when a lack of collaboration has caused unnecessary difficulties, do not hide the event, but use it as a learning opportunity to let everyone else know that certain behaviours are counterproductive.

Communication strategies

Having built the foundations of a collaborative culture, it must then be maintained. Some thought must be given early in the project cycle to the questions that arise around the word 'communication', and the strategies that need to be put in place to successfully exchange information, ideas and even feelings amongst the project participants and stakeholders. Every large project will have its own particular matrix of stakeholders, sponsors and team members whose connection to the project must be maintained. The problem with communication is that a leadership team can spend an almost unlimited amount of time undertaking activities that involve exchanging messages with people connected to the project. The hunger for information can, at times, seem insatiable. Communication is the one element of team performance feedback in which management and leadership will always be criticized. Part of the problem is that the term communication is too broad, as different individuals or groups want different types of information exchange at different stages in the project. There is also a separation between the needs of those working inside the project organization from those outside.

Internal communication

Looking first at internal communication strategies, it is useful to understand the escalating level of intensity of communication activity as one seeks to settle a team working in an uncertain environment. In steady state, the team has certain information needs from around the project it requires to perform its role. In most cases it can find much of this information itself. To build awareness and then engagement with the wider project, more information is needed for people to understand what is happening elsewhere and to find an emotional connection. In times of uncertainty, the desire for information increases, particularly if the project must go through some form of major structural change. The internal communication strategy should recognize the three primary categories of communication within organizations. Peter Robertson (2005) separates them into formal (written), direct (face-to-face) and informal (spoken).

Formal communication is usually contained in a written document. It is a record of what has been agreed or decided and has a degree of authority in that everyone can see the same document and, as such, it can be seen as the writer's version of the truth. Written communication is, however, often inadequate when trying to explain the implications of complexity.

Direct or face-to-face communication is regarded as having the biggest potential impact. Not only does this offer the opportunity to provide the audience with a formal statement of the reality at a particular moment in time but also it allows the use of non-verbal signals such as body language, facial expression and tone of voice. Direct communication can therefore convey a degree of emotion that adds context.

Informal communication is potentially the most influential, but can also be mis-directive. When people feel uncertain or feel they are missing information, they will seek out conversations with others who may be able to fill in the gaps. Humans place a high level of credibility on this unofficial information, which might otherwise be dismissed as 'gossip', particularly when it provides a degree of comfort or confirms our beliefs or suspicions.

Communication intensity might be measured in terms of the volume of messages being transmitted or in time spent in communication activities. Alternatively, intensity can be viewed as the amount of face-to-face conversations between team leaders and staff. There is no single formula for success, but it is worth taking on board the following principles:

1. Maintain the drum beat of the aligning narrative. In Chapter 3, I introduced the concept of an aligning narrative, which provides the underlying theme that should inform much of the early communication broadcast from the ILT. Chris Fussell (2017) describes the aligning narrative as a drum beat, whose repetition eventually becomes embedded in the minds of each

individual. When reflecting on the aligning narrative of the military intelligence taskforce in Iraq he comments:

> [T]his narrative, told to us every day, cast each of us as an actor in an entirely new story. We started to feel what was possible and the best among us were showing a willingness to forgo concepts of 'tribe' in order to become part of this new culture.

The aligning narrative should focus around the core principles that emerged from the set-up process. Choosing values that are actionable rather than subjective allows the leadership to craft messages that can be seen to have practical implications and will therefore make more sense. Cultural values often need to fight against the tribal and transactional instincts and so must be continually repeated, weekly or even daily to keep reinforcing the message that 'this is how we are going to work together to succeed'.

2. Make good use of stories that build upon the underlining narrative. Stories are the most effective mechanisms for transferring ideas experiences and lessons from one group to another. Recent advances in neuroscience have started to shed some light on why stories work as well as they do. When we listen to a story the parts of our brains that deal with language processing become activated to decode the meaning. This happens when we start to take in any form of new information, but when we hear a story our emotions also become aroused, stimulating a wider potential range of response. Feel-good chemicals such as serotonin, dopamine and oxytocin are produced as we react to thoughts that resonate with our own experiences. The effect is that we remember stories for much longer than we can recall bullet points in a PowerPoint presentation.

3. Avoid public relations 'fluff'. Too many project newsletters and bulletin boards focus solely on good news stories. Small successes and positive personal profiles are undoubtedly a useful and important tool in building wider team cohesion, but they often lose their value when they omit any reference to the challenges the teams may be facing. Bad news travels much faster than any formal communications process can work, so it is important to acknowledge problems and difficulties, even if a solution has yet to be found.

4. Remember the cultural principle that information passing through the teams should be plentiful rather than restricted. Leadership teams who try and control negative information are usually fooling themselves. In periods of difficulty and uncertainty, people will seek out their peers to find out the latest 'gossip'. Information quickly becomes distorted into a series of half-truths, which only serve to increase anxiety and reduce engagement.

5. Be as clear in your messages as possible. In uncertain times all ambiguous or neutral messages will be interpreted negatively. Trying to 'water down' difficult news is a waste of time. So if there is nothing to say, then don't say anything.

External communication

The other primary facet of communication is to maintain the support of the external bodies that have an interest in the project. Most projects begin with a high level of support from a number of key stakeholders. These are the people who have approved the resources or have a need for the project to succeed. As the project proceeds, conditions change and early assumptions often prove to be incorrect. If the programme extends and costs start to rise, there is a tendency for people to start to distance themselves from the project. There are, after all, few benefits in being associated with a failing project.

A critically important element of external engagement is to ensure that key stakeholders remain supportive by paying attention to a concept put forward by Karen Brown, Nancy Meyer and Richard Ettenson (2017) called the 'cycle of doubt'. The cycle is illustrated in Figure 6.1. They observe that when an event occurs in a project which triggers a degree of doubt in the mind of an important stakeholder, the consequence is that the reputation of the project declines slightly. This leads to a loss of support, which potentially reduces resources needed to deliver the project. This in turn means that more deadlines are missed and so there are further doubt triggers.

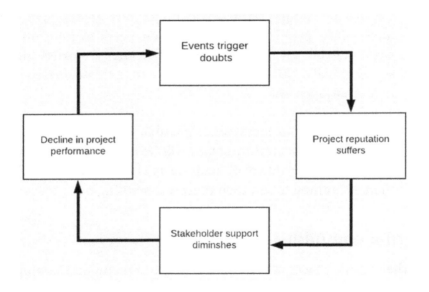

Figure 6.1 Illustration of the cycle of doubt

This might seem quite obvious, but the reality of the cycle is more subtle. The goals and objectives of the project remain in place, but once the project's reputation starts to decline the peripheral support needed from other parts of the organizations involved is now harder to secure. Resources become less easy to access and influential individuals start to distance themselves from the project. This leads to further problems as support is slowly withdrawn, continuing the cycle.

The *cycle of doubt* does not immediately kill your project. After all, doubt is not the same as disbelief or hostility. The effect is less of a collapse in confidence and more of a sense of decline. It is not that the stakeholders no longer believe in the project, but they slowly become more sceptical of the chances of success. Understanding the phenomenon of a slow withdrawal of support is important because it is often initially invisible in the early stages. Once the *cycle of doubt* takes hold, however, it can be difficult to reverse.

The point is to recognize a common tendency towards complacency when managing stakeholders. Consequently, stakeholder support is neglected until there is a crisis, by which time the *cycle of doubt* has set in and time must now be invested trying to rebuild the project's reputation. The lesson to absorb is that when your project starts to go off plan, stop the cycle of doubt by addressing issues early. Communicate openly and honestly with key stakeholders and continually work to maintain their confidence in your ability to deliver.

Meetings strategy

Before completing this chapter on engagement, I want to focus on the primary point of communication between sub-teams. People working in Big Teams will spend a lot of time connecting face-to-face (or by conference call) in what is generically called a meeting. This communication medium is an essential element of project life. We need to meet to pass on and collect information, to plan how to work together and so solve problems. The larger and more complex the project, the more time people must spend in meetings. Few people say they enjoy meetings and many would say they detest them.

The list of complaints about project meetings is long and remarkably consistent: too many people in attendance; no agenda; overrunning time; the wrong people in the room; no actions noted. I have heard the same complaints so many times, it occurs to me that project teams forget the basics of how to hold effective meetings. If one costed out the lost number of hours spent in meetings by the numerous participants on any large project, most leaders would be horrified at the expense. I therefore advocate the leadership team establishes a set of meeting rules that every team must adhere to. Following these rules will not necessarily make meetings more enjoyable, but will at least save time and reduce frustration.

Appoint a chair

Someone must take ownership of the efficiency of the meeting. The role of the chair is to ensure that the meeting fulfils its purpose, holds to the agenda, sticks to time and ensures that next actions are agreed. The chair is not necessarily the most senior person in the room. It should be treated as a distinct role that benefits from an agreed process, and some training in basic chairing skills. This might seem a bit too controlling. After all, how difficult is it to chair a meeting? My response is that chairing a meeting effectively is a skilled process and the skills need to be learned. If you are unconvinced, imagine a Big Team holding thousands of meetings all being chaired effectively based on a common approach, and contrast that thought with the same number of randomly managed meetings. Which option is going to be the most productive?

Agree an agenda

A meeting needs structure so that everyone knows what they should be focusing on. If an agenda has not been formally issued before the meeting, the first action in the meeting is to agree:

1. What do we need to talk about today?
2. What actions do we need to agree to?

The agenda sets the sequence and progression of the discussion and is, in effect, a form of contract between the attendees on where they must concentrate their attention. People's attention falls away as they tire so deal with the most important topics first and allow procedural items to fall down the agenda. For this reason, I dislike the old-fashioned procedure of reviewing the minutes of the previous meeting (assuming some have been taken). This practice is a hangover from the 20th century when most business meetings were essentially a form of committee where procedure was regarded as more important than impact, and meeting time was plentiful.

The right people in the room

There is a rule of thumb that the more people you have around a meeting room table, the longer and less effective the meeting will be. Other than update meetings where a large group is assembled to be presented with a progress report, try to limit the number of attendees to no more than seven or eight people. Any more and you will find that half the room stays silent whilst conversation is dominated by a few individuals. Eight seems to be the number that allows everyone to engage in discussion and to feel a sense of ownership of the issues under discussion.

This is, of course, easier said than done, as big projects tend to create a need to assemble representatives from every sub-team. The result is large, unwieldly sessions that make slow progress and become procedural. There is a paradox here in that, on the one hand, I hear people complain about how dull big procedural meetings tend to be but, on the other hand, they would feel offended if not invited to attend. The golden rule is to ask the attendees 'why are you here?' If it is simply to be aware of what is going on, then tell them to read the minutes and go spend their time more productively. This might seem somewhat authoritarian but if you can instil that question in everyone's mind as a matter of habit, you will not only free up time in people's diaries, but will also get a more focused discussion from those whose intent is to provide some input into the discussion.

Timing

Get into the habit of starting the meeting on time, irrespective of whether everyone has arrived or not. I have noticed over the years that internal meetings where people are based in the same building fall into a routine where it is acceptable to arrive 10 minutes late, on the basis that no one else turns up on time. This is a chronic waste of resource, particularly if one only has a limited time slot. One of the curses of a modern project is for senior people to find their diaries fully booked with back-to-back meetings. Once one session overruns then every following meeting starts to run late. For this reason, another good habit is for the chair to start winding the meeting up 5–10 minutes before the scheduled end time. If the meeting needs to run over, it is a conscious decision, and the consequences on following meetings are understood.

Agree actions

Another surprising complaint I frequently hear is that a meeting takes place, usually focused on a problem or issue, and everyone leaves with a different version in their minds as to what has been agreed. Problem-solving meetings should be summarized towards the end, and the next actions agreed and noted. This is not optional.

Notes

Related to the problem of a lack of common understanding is the lack of notes or minutes. In small meetings of peers, someone needs to take notes. Since this is a role few people enjoy, the task falls to the most junior person in the room. This is a problem, however, if they lack the experience to understand the nuances of what is being discussed. Taking notes, even if it is just an agreed set of actions, should be owned by the most senior person round the table, even if they do not do the writing. The point is that in a large project, every decision made by one team will have an effect somewhere else in the project so a record of what has been discussed and decided must be available to inform other teams of the potential implications.

Space

Teams need space to meet, and the larger the project the more meeting spaces that are required. There never seems to be enough space. When planning the layout of any project office accommodation, give some serious thought to the balance of space allocated between meeting rooms and desk space. Even when space is limited, consider giving priority to meeting space over workstations. When I walk around an office designed to hold a large project team, I often find over half of the workstations are unattended. If you ask where the people are, the invariable answer is that 'they are in a meeting'!

Summary

Maintaining full team engagement should be a proactive rather than reactive process. This means that someone at a senior level needs to own responsibility for planning team engagement activity, and resources need to be included in the budget to implement those plans. Once again, this requires a step change in the thinking needed as one moves from a 'normal' complicated project to a large complex one. Containing the forces of behavioural gravity is not a hypothetical challenge, so having plans and processes in place to keep the teams motivated and energized will save you a considerable amount of time that would otherwise be spent unravelling avoidable problems. The question then is how do you know how your teams are feeling? The simple answer is to ask them. This leads us nicely to the next chapter.

Chapter 7
Feedback and behavioural risk

We should by now have established the concept that the performance of a Big Team is reliant on the ability to learn and develop as the project moves from set-up into task delivery. To reach the performance standards that are going to be needed to maintain the pace required in modern projects, the teams must seek out the most effective learning tool available, which is generally known as *feedback*.

The concept of feedback comes from the world of cybernetics and the idea that outputs from a system create data, which can then be fed back into the system to help regulate itself. In the world of projects, feedback is an invaluable mechanism to assess the extent to which a team is proceeding in line with its plans. This information is potentially available in the form of objective data, such as numerical measurements of time and cost, or as subjective data based on perception and opinion. It is this more subjective element of feedback that concerns us when considering human performance. The process provides a team with the data it needs to be able to regulate itself so that it can:

- identify processes that are not working;
- assess and improve competency;
- correct negative behaviours;
- reinforce positive team attributes;
- improve communication and collaboration skills; and
- identify and adapt to changing circumstances.

Such information should be regarded as invaluable to any team that is conscious of a need to develop and improve. Yet few teams seem able to adopt the mindset that welcomes criticism of its individual or collective abilities.

The willingness to collect subjective data, analyse and then use the data to correct or change behaviours is a cultural challenge. Many experienced individuals avoid being assessed and tend to be brittle when faced with criticism. This often reflects a lack of confidence in certain areas, particularly when taking feedback on the softer attributes of management. Few projects are set up with a feedback system ready from day one. I have seen a wide range of staff questionnaires, 360 appraisal forms and team temperature checks. Many major projects commission some form of feedback survey, often about six to nine months from the start of the project. Such exercises often tend to be done on an ad hoc basis with little clear thought as to how the data will be used, and as such have limited direct value in improving team performance.

Feedback data are too valuable to be treated as an afterthought, and should be incorporated in the delivery process framework from the start. Teams should collect data on themselves monthly, or even weekly. The leadership team should be collecting additional data providing not just for performance but, just as importantly, to monitor and manage behavioural risk.

Monitoring behavioural risk

In an uncertain world, the desire to mitigate or reduce risk is a growing component of the project management process. There is an increased recognition that the traditional approach to risk management via the creation of a risk register has many limitations. The problem is that the traditional concept of risk is typically constrained by a narrow focus on technical risk (will the project actually do what it is supposed to?) or commercial risk (will it take longer and/or cost more than planned?). The reality of project life is that the technical and commercial elements only reflect a part of the project dynamic. As discussed throughout this book, people tend to be one of the more unpredictable factors, posing their own element of risk to the performance of the project. Behavioural risk can be defined as those risks that are associated with the judgements and decisions that are flawed, either because of a lack of information or a misinterpretation of the data available to an individual or a group. Or to put it another way, it is the risk arising when the people involved in your project do not behave in the way you expect them to.

Ralph Stacey (2003), one of the pre-eminent thinkers in the world of complex project management, makes a very useful observation that problems within projects are often subjective and interpersonal, resulting from a team of people working uncertainly towards a certain goal with emergent complex team behaviours. In other words, it is not the technical or commercial challenges that often derail projects but the people who must try to work together to find the solutions. It therefore makes sense to add human behaviour into the risk equation.

Early-warning signals

This leads us to the concept of early-warning signals (EWSs). Williams et al. (2012, p. 38) use a definition provided by I. O. Nikander (2010) who defines an EWS as:

> An observation, message or some other form of communication that is, or can be seen as, an expression, indication or proof or the existence of some future or incipient positive or negative issue. It is a signal, an omen or an indication of future developments.

The use of the word 'omen' is interesting, in that it is not commonly used in the context of managing a project. An omen is a portent of what may happen rather than an accurate prediction, and is based on a sense rather than hard facts. The idea of making decisions based on a feeling that cannot be backed up with precise data is counter-intuitive to our professional training. And yet looking at the evidence from so many project failures, it is clear that we need to take more notice of the weak signals that are available when events start to move in an unplanned direction. Analysis of unsuccessful projects frequently shows that the signs of impending disaster were available well in advance of the final failure. The hard facts that confirm a warning tend to arrive just before the crisis hits, when there is no time available to take preventive action.

There is therefore a very strong case for making better use of the data that EWSs can provide. So how do EWSs fit within the traditional approach to project risk management? The answer is not as easily as they should. Risk management on major projects tends to maintain a focus within the project bubble. The risk identification process focus tends to be on technical issues based on an awareness of incomplete information. A typical risk register therefore comprises a schedule of 'known unknowns'. On major projects, disruption often comes from outside the technical domain, usually manifested by human interaction (or the lack thereof).

This limited perspective of project risk once again illustrates the potential problems arising from an orange-stage mindset that sees a project as a controllable mechanistic process. Green-stage thinking views risk through the three core perspectives of technical, commercial and behavioural. Using these three lenses provides an holistic overview of risk by recognizing that the three elements are interconnected rather than being regarded as distinct risk categories. Project teams therefore need to learn to scan the horizon, looking for a wider range of signals that may indicate trouble ahead. The challenge is not to limit the awareness of risk to rational measurements and facts but to also learn to recognize signals that emanate from our other senses.

Cultural barriers

Based on the above observations, it should be a simple matter of good project governance to establish a process or system to collect EWSs. Logic, however, is not enough. The studies that have been done around EWSs reveal that picking up the signals is only part of the task. Recognizing the available data and then taking action on the information provided is often a greater challenge. If the signs of impending disaster are frequently available to us, why do so many teams choose to ignore them? As is so often the case, it is partly down to poor systems, but more often is the result of human fallibility.

A study by Igor Ansoff (1984) identified the phenomenon that data often need to pass through a number of filters before coming to the attention of senior decision makers. As illustrated in Figure 7.1, a message coming from within, or around, the project environment must first pass through a *surveillance* filter. In other words, someone actually needs to notice the signal. To be processed, the message must then pass through a *mentality* filter, which sets out what kind of information an individual or organization deems to be important. The final filter is the *political/power* filter, which decides whether or not the information created by the signal should be allowed to influence how decisions are made. These psychological filters are subconscious rather than explicit, and will be largely unrecognized by the project team until they are drawn to their attention. It is therefore a useful exercise for leadership teams to question their personal and cultural filters and acknowledge where they might be ignoring information that is signalling problems ahead.

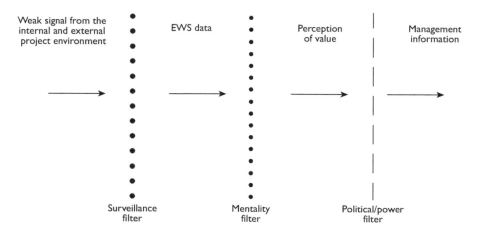

Figure 7.1 Message filtering process (adapted from Ansoff 1984)

Another study by Terry Williams et al. (2012) concluded that humans are generally not very good at picking up the EWSs that might affect a project. They point to three key areas where project leaders often struggle:

1. A limited understanding on the full scope of project risk.
2. A low recognition of the implications of project complexity.
3. A lack of the significance given to tacit/unwritten information shared between people, and how they react and respond to such communication.

Each of these three areas merits consideration, but for the purposes of this chapter we will focus on the third point concerning the people-oriented, or social aspects, of activity happening within and around a major project. Many of the barriers to the effective use of EWSs can be seen to be cultural rather than organizational blockages, as illustrated in Table 7.1.

Table 7.1 Examples of behavioural blockages to the use of EWSs

Limiting factor	*Behavioural blockage*
Internal politics	The extent to which only certain information is presented at board level, ignoring soft issues and focusing instead on hard data, particularly time and cost.
Optimism bias	Avoiding discussion of potential problems in the belief the issue will probably resolve itself.
Discomfort with conflict	A low desire by management to deal with interpersonal issues before they break into open conflict.
Shooting the messenger	A tendency by senior management to react negatively on hearing unexpected bad news, who, instead of accepting the information as valid, are critical of the person highlighting the problem.

Lack of faith in the response	A reluctance to raise potential issues with management in the belief that no action will be taken and so identifying an issue is a waste of effort.
Rejection of external input	Rejection of observations from outside of the team or organization on the grounds that as an external party their views have secondary validity to those within the project.

These points illustrate a major challenge to the project leadership team and should ideally be discussed early in the project lifecycle. Does your team believe that a process for identifying and collecting EWSs would be valuable? If so, can you recognize the cultural and mental filters that will limit your ability to receive information and then act on it? Most rational leaders would say yes, confident in the belief that they would not be so blind to such potentially valuable data. It is important to recognize, however, that the cultural and systemic forces that limit our thinking are strong and are often subconscious. Breaking through these limitations requires a degree of effort. This can be illustrated by our reactions to signals coming from 'gut feel'.

Learning to value 'gut feel'

I have written elsewhere on the value of gut feel in anticipating risk. Quoting from a section in a previous publication (Llewellyn & Moore 2019, p. 201):

Human beings are wired to seek out to danger. In the modern workplace, we are rarely concerned about physical safety. Our mental and physiological systems nevertheless remain programmed to watch and listen for signs of any threat to ourselves, or our tribe. We often first pick up the sense of such threats in our stomach. Put simplistically, if we feel under threat, a part of the brain releases chemicals which can often be felt as contractions in our gut. Hence the phrase. Gut feel can be stimulated by little more than watching the reactions or body language of another team member. You might notice a small response to a peripheral issue that feels too remote to be a real problem and yet is still bothering you. It can often be difficult to articulate these feelings. How do you write down a rational explanation based on a tightening in your stomach? And yet the studies are clear that our gut instincts are often an accurate predictor of trouble ahead.

It should be acknowledged that someone having a difficult day and feeling pessimistic is not necessarily an EWS. A lot of people feeling pessimistic at the same time however is another matter. One of the benefits of having a large number of people involved in a major project is the facility to tap into the 'wisdom of crowds'. In his book on the subject, James Suroweicki (2005) makes a valid proposition that groups of individuals will make better aggregated decisions than lone subject-matter experts. Collecting weak signals from as wide a group as possible can allow you to spot trends early. It is easy to dismiss one person's concerns about a particular problem based on gut feel, but when ten people express a similar sense, it could be important.

The technique is to design a process to pick up data that are quick to collect, easy to analyse and that the contributors believe will be valuable. In the following section I have set out some ideas for creating your own project-specific EWS process. As pointed out above, the investment in building a system to collect these valuable data will be wasted if your team's mental filters reject the information before it has a chance to be considered. However, if you have the foresight and perception to work through these cultural constraints, you will give yourself a much greater chance of managing your project through the maze of complexity and uncertainty.

A PRACTICAL EXAMPLE OF AN EWS IN ACTION

To illustrate how behavioural risk might be monitored, I offer an example of a multi-million pound residential scheme being planned for a large site in North London. The site put a lot of constraints on the design as it had to deal with difficult underground conditions as well as being subject to strict planning criteria. The wider team has ranged between 100 and 150 people over the two-year design period, from an extensive range of design and development backgrounds. They had to work through a number of gateways to get sponsor approval, and the environment had been quite pressured. The client had taken an active approach to risk management since the start, and initially appointed a risk manager who took the team down the traditional risk register route. Having learned from previous projects that the human factor can derail the best plans, they also commissioned an online system that monitored the progress of a series of behavioural indicators on a bi-monthly basis.

In line with the above principles, the questions covered areas that indicate alignment, engagement and resilience within the different sub-teams. These included an assessment of issues such as adequate resourcing, communication, coordination, team morale, project complexity and effective meetings. These indicators were expressed as a point on a sliding scale, but the system also provided the opportunity to identify any specific concerns using open text. The responses were sent out to the whole team, to coincide with the project leadership meetings, and were collated by a third party to allow for anonymity. The resulting report was then presented to the project leadership team, who then agreed a course of action to respond to any issues that could be managed at that time. It was interesting to note how the indicators moved over a 12-month period, so that as alignment and engagement improved, so did the team's productivity as measured by the ability to deliver to specific milestones.

Creating hard data to manage the soft stuff

The secret to managing behavioural risk lies in taking a systemic approach, which requires looking beyond the immediate symptoms of a problem and instead looking deeper to understand what is happening in the wider project environment that is influencing human behaviour. Whilst we all have our individual quirks and preferences, we tend to react to our circumstances in a surprisingly consistent manner. For example, when people feel threatened or disrespected they will typically disengage from the situation leading to a drop in the care and attention that they would otherwise pay to their work. A root cause analysis of failure or disruption in a project can often be traced back to three common factors:

- A lack of alignment of the project team where individuals have different objectives to those of the sponsor or stakeholder.
- A lack of engagement with the project leading to lower levels of commitment and minimal creative problem-solving.
- A lack of resilience in the team as pressure from repeated deadlines and a lack of capable resources increase stress, reduce productivity and increase the likelihood of errors.

It does not take much imagination to recognize that if a portion of your project team feels stressed and disengaged, just when you are relying on them to be energized and committed, then behavioural problems are likely to occur. In small project teams it is possible to notice when the group is not functioning as a cohesive unit. As the project team grows and splits into a number of sub-teams, then you need to start collecting data to allow you to monitor which parts of the team are aligned, engaged and show signs of resilience.

The simplest way to monitor signs of behavioural risk is to create some form of feedback tool, usually in the form of a questionnaire, which collects data on those aspects of a project that are likely to affect levels of alignment, engagement and resilience. These will vary according to the particular phase of the project cycle and so there is no standard list.

Common factors include budgetary constraints, realistic programmes, communication strategies, client/sponsor experience, clarity of scope and physical working conditions. Each of these elements will have an impact on how a team of individuals reacts when working alongside each other.

There are a range of web-based tools that can help you collect data. Successful mitigation requires identifying the appropriate behavioural risk and then monitoring on a regular basis. It is better to collect small amounts of data on a regular basis than to do periodic temperature tests that ask too many questions. Every group of individuals assembled to work as a team will be unique in the way they think, behave and interact with others. It is consequently easy to come to the view that human behaviours are too 'soft' to be of use to a management team used to making decisions on hard facts. However, our behaviours typically show a level of consistency to allow them to be monitored. The technique is not to try and measure behaviours themselves, but instead look at those factors that are likely to cause a change in behaviours.

When measuring any activity, it is worth understanding what you are trying to achieve. Gathering and processing data takes time and energy, so it is worth being clear what you will do with the output. The day-to-day behaviours you see in your team are likely to be a reaction to the circumstances surrounding them, and the extent to which they feel psychologically safe. Ideally your team is working together as an open, flexible, trusting and resilient unit. You should therefore try to monitor those factors that are known to heavily influence the perception of the team environment. You may feel that perception is an imprecise measure, but actually this is the point of the exercise. In any given situation, a group of people may look at the facts presented to them, and each come to a different conclusion as to what they mean. By asking a series of questions on a regular basis, you can get feedback on the resilience of the team and the extent to which everyone is 'on the same page'.

Methodology

Building a process for measuring behavioural key performance indicators (KPIs) need not be complicated. Here are some tips that may help.

1. Before you start, get buy-in to the idea from the team. The larger the project, the more that early buy-in is important. Once you have gained their agreement in principle, it is much harder to argue against the practical need to take time to provide the data, and then to receive the results.

2. Decide on the mechanism for collecting the data. For small teams of ten or fewer, this might be done using a spreadsheet. As the team size grows, you could use an online survey tool. For larger project teams of 25 or more, it is worth exploring proprietary feedback systems that can automatically collate the data making it easier to create a management report.

3. Decide on the period between each exercise. On short but intense projects this might be done weekly. On larger projects you might do the exercise at monthly or six-weekly intervals. The point is to collect data that allow you to see trends.

4. Agree what questions to ask. A simple mechanism is to ask each member the extent to which the participants agree with a number of statements. You can make these very specific to the project, but there are a number of areas that are consistently found to impact on team performance. Some examples are listed below:
   - Clear strategy – The strategy for delivering this project is absolutely clear to me.
   - Trust – The culture of the team encourages open admission of weaknesses and mistakes.

- Respect – I feel that team members consistently treat each other respectfully.
- Roles and responsibilities – I am clear on the roles and responsibilities that each member of the team plays in the delivery of this project.
- No blame culture – I see a culture in the team of trying to learn from problems rather than apportion blame.
- Flexibility – I often see examples of flexibility in the team's approach.
- Meetings – All of our meetings are compelling, well-structured and productive.

5. Decide how to collect and process the data. There is an advantage in finding an independent individual to sort the information and produce the report. This might incur some additional cost, but the safer the team feel about raising concerns, the better quality of information is likely to be fed back.

6. Agree when/how to bring the condensed information back to the team to discuss and, where necessary, take action.

Summary

Technical people are typically more comfortable dealing with technical issues, and would generally prefer not to have to deal with the challenges presented by people and their messy emotions. The problem with behavioural data is that is that you may not like what you are being told. Feedback that is critical of the management team is not always welcome. The team's instinctive reaction to unfavourable news may be to try ignore it, dispute its credibility or blame the person or group who produced the report.

Much depends upon your perspective. Would you prefer to know that there were difficulties brewing before they become problematic or just deal with the issues when they blow up into a crisis? Rationally, most project managers would like advance warning but history consistently shows that we quickly become defensive when we feel threatened by criticism. It may therefore take a bit of effort to ensure that the team moves beyond its initial instinctive reactions, and recognizes the value that critical data has in helping the team adjust its behaviours and regain cohesion.

There is always a potential danger of the team suffering from feedback fatigue. Collecting information on the issues that affect team behaviours provides the team with a formal outlet, which is not otherwise easily available to them. If they feel their input is ignored then they are less likely to contribute in the future. If you are going to ask your team for their thoughts and observations, then you must also be prepared to take action when the issues are important.

A final recommendation is to be patient and stick with the process. It typically takes three to four iterations before the team gets used to the data collecting and reporting process. The data become useful when you aggregate the statistics and can follow trends. If your scores in any one area are dropping, even by a small amount over three iterations, you have probably got an issue that needs exploring.

Collecting and managing behavioural data is a time-consuming process. Whilst parts of it can be automated or even outsourced, as project leader you must still pay attention to what the data are telling you. Traditional KPIs such as programme and cost only tell you a part of the story. Adding the behavioural dimension will give a more complete picture of what is really happening on the project.

Chapter 8
Building resilience

Every major project is likely to go through periods where events do not go as planned. Going back to the discussion on complexity in the first chapter, no project can exist in isolation from the conditions surrounding it. Changes in the political or economic climate can lead to significant shifts in stakeholder support, increasing pressure on time and budget. Within the project bubble there are also likely to be problems, as unexpected technical difficulties cause delays and increase costs. In a complex environment, there are so many potential hurdles and pitfalls that it is not possible to plan for every potential crisis. The best mitigation strategy is to build teams that are resilient and equipped to adjust, adapt and continue to perform in changing conditions.

Resilience can be defined as the capacity to recover quickly from difficulties. The term is often associated with words such as toughness, hardiness and strength. The danger in such terms is they can perpetuate the idea that pressure and stress are problems that are best ignored, and all that is really required is to muddle through. The stoic philosophy of enduring pain and hardship without showing any emotion is respected in most cultures, until someone reaches the point of exhaustion when everything then collapses. Rather than leave the resilience of the team to chance, it is a better strategy to enable your team not only to survive the buffeting winds of change but also to thrive on the experience.

Resilience has become one of the 'buzz words' of the 21st century as commentators, authors and researchers try to reconcile the shifting patterns of activity with a human desire to minimize uncertainty. A wide range of literature has been published in recent years on individual resilience and, at a higher level, organizational resilience. There has, however, been relatively little scientific research into team resilience. The few papers that have attempted to study team resilience find there

is, not surprisingly, a direct relationship between resilience and social
cohesion within a team (Meneghel et al. 2016; Gittel et al. 2006; Riolli
& Savicki 2003).

Michael West (2012), one of the leading academics in the field of
effective teamwork, provides a simple but useful model to illustrate the
interplay between two of the dominant aspects of task focus and social
cohesion. As illustrated in Figure 8.1, teams with a high task focus and
high social cohesion are likely to be more resilient than teams with high
task focus but low social cohesion. West observes that *resilient* teams
tend to pay attention both to high task effectiveness and to member
well-being. The effect is to stimulate high inter-team cooperation and
enhance long-term viability. By contrast, a *driven* team may have high
short-term task effectiveness, but low attention to member well-being
tends to stimulate inter-team conflict and reduces the team's ability to
innovate.

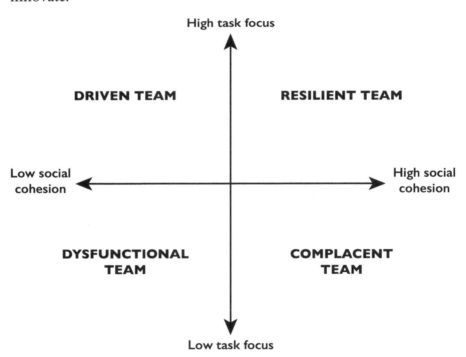

Figure 8.1 Resilient vs driven teams (adapted from West 2012)

A paper written by George Allinger and his colleagues (2015) identifies five markers of team resilience to illustrate the difference between a resilient team and a brittle team:

1. Resolution of problems. Acknowledging and addressing issues as quickly as possible, rather than allowing decisions to drift.
2. Team health. Paying attention to coordination, cohesion and morale sustains energy and willingness to tackle difficult problems. It also reduces internal conflict.
3. Resources. The accumulation and maintenance of both technical and emotional resources during periods of pressure, rather than allowing them to drain away leaving the team depleted.
4. Recovery. The ability to 'bounce back' after a challenging experience rather than continuing through a period of diminished effectiveness.
5. Ongoing viability. Resilient teams manage resources to maintain viability and are ready to meet the next challenge. Brittle teams who are slow to recover represent a greater risk to the viability of the project.

The message that comes through from the research is that social cohesion and the maintenance of a supportive environment are key to the development of team resilience. This might seem a little obvious, but it goes against the perceived wisdom that resilience sits with the individual rather than the team. There is a logic that to build a resilient team, you just need to fill it with resilient people. There is undoubtedly some truth in this train of thought, but it depends upon how you define a resilient person.

PREPARING FOR THE STORM

To illustrate a structured approach to building team resilience I offer a case story based on the crews sailing around the globe as part of the annual Clipper Round the World Yacht Race. The tribulations of a crew of an ocean-going yacht may seem remote from the challenges of a desk-bound team trying to survive organizational upheaval. As you will see, however, the ocean provides some useful metaphors for the challenge teams must face in any conditions where endurance and willpower are required.

The sea is a great example of an unpredictable environment: exciting to some, petrifying to others. There are, of course, some key differences to 'normal' life. Taking part in an ocean-going race is a physically demanding activity, in which the competitors make a voluntary choice to take part. Most humans enjoy the sensation of the smooth motion of a boat moving through calm water. Once out of harbour, however, there is no getting off and walking away when the sea gets rough. The experiences of a racing crew provide many interesting parallels to a team working through a difficult challenge. The crew have a common goal, and require strong leadership, not just from the skipper, but also his/her lieutenants. The team members need to be compatible and have the mix of skills that are required to achieve their objective. They need to learn how to work effectively together and must build trust in each other.

Living on a clipper yacht is physically uncomfortable, sleep can be erratic and the process of keeping the boat travelling at speed requires continuous high levels of concentration. Sailing on a yacht with 20 other people over long distances therefore compresses and amplifies the team experience. To be allowed to take part in the race an aspiring crew member must pass four levels of training to make sure they have a basic technical grasp of most areas of the boat. This training does not, however, really prepare them for some of the experiences that they will face, such as the onslaught of 115 knots of wind gusting through in the North Pacific, or the big swells of the Southern Ocean.

Sailing across an ocean is a 24-hour operation, so it is not like a normal 8- or 9-hour day in the office. A typical day is 6 hours on and 6 hours off during the day, and then 4-hour shifts at nights. It is very tiring both physically and mentally, particularly in periods of sleep deprivation. The crews typically develop routines where they continually review and improve. So, for example, every time they complete an 'evolution', such as a sail change or putting a reef in the main sail, they debrief in terms of what worked well, and how they can improve, be quicker or more accurate. The mindset is that one never stops learning whether one is experienced or not, so they always debrief.

The payoff comes in an emergency. I was given an example of an incident on the first leg across the Atlantic where a crew had a call for 'all hands on deck' because the halyard sail had broken and was trapped under the boat. The incident was in the middle of the night so everyone was woken to help try to drag the sail up from under the boat. There was a degree of panic at first, especially for the people who had been asleep and didn't know what was going on. It was pitch black and so they couldn't see, but nevertheless they quickly fell into the drills they had been trained to perform. The morning after, the crew expressed a degree of amazement at how quickly they became able to work as a team to solve the crisis.

Resilient behaviours

Taking an image from the entertainment world, one might picture a resilient individual who is physically and mentally tough, who can withstand pain and who will drive themselves on regardless of personal discomfort. This is the image of the hero who comes through adversity based on qualities of 'grit' and determination. In reality, having a team of such rugged individuals would probably not be very effective as they tend to be 'outsiders' who value independence and dislike having to rely on others to succeed. There are, however, individual characteristics that you might seek when assembling a team that will need to be resilient. A study by Hendrie Weisinger and J. P. Pawliw-Fry (2015) picked out ten of the most common resilient behaviours observed by those who worked with them. These behaviours are summarized below:

1. Are not defensive when criticized.
2. Stay calm under pressure.
3. Handle setbacks effectively.
4. Manage anxiety stress, anger and fear in pursuit of goal.
5. Use criticism and other feedback for growth.
6. Show a positive outlook.
7. Maintain a sense of humour.
8. Can see things from another's perspective.
9. Recognize the effect of their behaviour on others.
10. Are able to discuss grievances skilfully.

These qualities align closely to the behaviours one would expect to find in a strong team, and provide a checklist to work with as part of a team development programme. The above behaviours are examples of abilities to manage emotions in difficult or uncomfortable situations rather than allowing them to dominate. These resilient behaviours can be learned and developed, particularly if a team is working in a psychologically safe environment.

Joseph McCann and John Selsky (2012) argue, however, that resilience alone is not sufficient and that to work through serious disruption, organizations and teams must also be agile. They define agility as 'the capacity for moving quickly, flexibly and decisively in anticipating, initiating and taking advantage of opportunities and avoiding the negative consequences of change' (2012, p. 19). This is an important observation, in that resilience in itself could be seen as a passive ability that helps the team survive a period of turbulence, but does not subsequently move the project on to another level. The authors point out that agility in itself is not enough to cope with a turbulent environment. Agile teams often structure themselves around lean cost structures and flexible resources, which can create fragility in a team when operating conditions intensify beyond their capacity to cope. The aim should therefore be to build adaptive capacity where the amount of resources and skills possessed by the team can maintain growth and viability relative to the requirements posed by the environment.

Kutsch, Hall and Turner (2015) reinforce this point in their work on the topic of resilient projects. They see a separation between project leaders who try to manage risk using a rule-based approach and those who instead seek to manage uncertainty based around the use of *mindfulness*. The problem they see in a rule-based approach is the tendency to limit how a problem is perceived so that it fits the process, rather than trying to understand what is happening and respond accordingly. The traditional rule-based approach to risk management is based on a process of forecasting, assessing, planning and then preventing. In contrast, the mindfulness approach uses mechanisms for noticing, interpreting, preparing and containing. The authors make the case that in a volatile and unpredictable climate, the traditional reliance on processes designed to try to control risk are likely to be too slow and inflexible to allow decision makers to react in time to minimize the impact of a crisis. The mindfulness philosophy pushes a leadership team to be agile, reflecting the sense-and-react approach adopted by green-stage teams.

A model of team resilience

The final section of this chapter sets out a model designed to help build both agility and resilience into a Big Team. The model is derived from the research supporting the other elements of Big Team development set out in the previous chapters. Teams that are set up to work as cohesive units will learn to focus on the importance of the social and behavioural aspects that lead to resilience. This extends into the recognition of the value of setting up feedback systems that enable teams to anticipate and prepare for periods of difficulty. Having a distinct resilience model, however, allows for the fact that projects move through numerous cycles and iterations over an extended period of time. Irrespective of the time invested in setting the initial framework for alignment and engagement, many of the processes that shape and influence team behaviours will need to be revisited. The model therefore has six stages that can be seen to work in a cycle as shown in Figure 8.2.

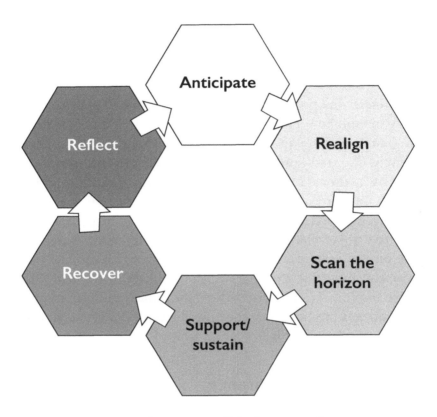

Figure 8.2 Six-step model of team resilience

Anticipate

In the context of a Big Team, anticipation is a process of maintaining awareness of problems and difficulties that are as yet unknown but nevertheless have the potential to occur. Given our previous discussions on complexity and uncertainty, this might appear to be a statement of the obvious. The analyses of project failure nevertheless frequently identify situations that caught a team by surprise. With hindsight, however, the signals of an impending crisis were often available but were still ignored. Beware of the natural tendency towards complacency, particularly when the project appears to be progressing as planned. Complacency tends to occur when we only focus on what is working and ignore aspects of the team's processes and behaviours that are suboptimal.

Complacency can also emerge when project performance metrics focus primarily on backward-looking measures. Orange-stage teams can place too much value on lagging indicators, because they tend to be easy to measure, but they are not necessarily useful predictors of what is likely to happen in the future. Anticipation requires the team to identify a number of leading indicators that are likely to have an effect on the project in the next three to six months.

Anticipation also requires a continual awareness as to what is happening outside of the project bubble. Watching for signals of change or tension in the sponsor's organization, as well as broader shifts in the political and social environments, should become a part of the leadership agenda. In practical terms, anticipation can be seen as a high-level exercise in risk management. Rather than focus on technical risk, anticipation is largely about creating the right mindset in leaders and managers to acknowledge that problems are likely to arise, and to take steps to be as well prepared as possible. It is a process of mental acknowledgement that problems are likely to occur, and that the views and concerns of others in the team are likely to be as valid in identifying signals of future disruption as those of the leadership group.

A useful exercise in anticipation is to carry out a 'pre-mortem'. This is an alternative approach to risk management where one assembles a wide group of people in a workshop format and asks them to imagine a period after the project has been completed but has not been successful. The question to the room is 'what went wrong?' Whilst a pre-mortem could be seen as another form of risk management, there is a key difference. Traditional risk management exercises are a rational process, based on an extrapolation of a logical sequence of events. A pre-mortem allows the participants to move beyond rational thinking and articulate concerns for which there may yet be no clear evidence, but are nevertheless potentially very real to the project participants. A case study on the use of a pre-mortem can be found at http:// teamcoachingtoolkit.com/the-pre-mortem/

Realign

The next element in building resilience is to check for alignment. Individuals and sub-teams will occasionally fall out of alignment, either because of changes in personnel or workflow. There is a benefit therefore in periodically working with the sub-teams to test their alignment, based around the following questions:

- Are all team members clear on the goals and objectives of the project?
- Do the espoused project values match up with the reality of day-to-day operations?
- Do the team members have Level Two relationships with each other, and with key individuals in other teams?
- Are the team's rules of engagement being adhered to?
- Are roles and accountabilities clear and unambiguous?
- Does the team regularly take time to reflect and learn?
- Is feedback regularly requested, analysed and actions taken?

The above list provides a basis for a questionnaire that can be adapted to suit the stage of the project. It would be highly unusual if the responses to these questions were unremittingly positive. As discussed above, human relationships in groups have a tendency towards dysfunction as relationships become strained by the forces of behavioural gravity. The key point here is to take steps to realign the team, reacting to low-scoring areas by revisiting the set-up framework described in Chapter 4.

Revisiting a team's alignment is an exercise that should be done on a regular basis, not just for the sub-teams but, perhaps more critically, for the leadership team as well. It can often be difficult to find time to take stock, but this short review helps avoid the dangers of complacency and will often help a team get back on track when performance has started to dip.

It should be noted that disruptive crises do not always occur as a result of dramatic events. Perhaps more insidious are the problems that arise from chronic, low-level challenges that emerge when some aspects of the wider team are out of alignment. Allinger et al. (2015) point out that challenges such a poor physical environment, ambiguous team roles or lingering conflict may not be recognized, or may not be seen as important enough to be addressed. These types of minor stressors can drain the team's 'battery', depleting energy and reducing performance to minimum acceptable levels. Even worse, this gradual shift to poor performance becomes normalized so that new members of the team are quickly caught up in a negative sub-culture which can then be difficult to reverse.

Scan the horizon

'Scanning the horizon' is a metaphor that calls for attention to focus on the near future and look for weak signals of trouble ahead. The process and mechanisms for horizon scanning are set out in Chapter 7. In line with the theme of mindfulness, anticipation should be part methodical review of feedback data and part 'gut feel'. Kutsch et al. (2015) use the term 'the art of noticing' to emphasize that resilience management is more about tapping into human senses than the scientific analysis of numerical data. They acknowledge the need to collect data, but make the case for extending the participants asked for input beyond a close group of technical experts to bring in observations from as broad a scope as possible. By encouraging every person who has an active role in the project to provide feedback, the team can build a rich set of data that is likely to reveal multiple perspectives.

I would reiterate the point that the signs of potential trouble tend to be visible long in advance of a crisis, but we are often too absorbed in our own day-to-day problems to take sufficient notice. Horizon scanning should therefore be a part of the leadership team resilience strategy, periodically revisited to consider what potential issues are within sight but have yet to have an impact.

Part of 'the art of noticing' is to identify the early stages of conflict between the sub-teams. It is useful to make the distinction between disagreement (potentially good), dispute (often normal) and conflict (usually destructive). Disagreement should be regarded as a potentially positive feature. Analysis of project failure frequently highlights the lack of challenges to bad decisions from within teams. A culture of non-confrontation means that they suffer from a lack of options arising from 'groupthink'. Effective teams often rely on disagreement to stimulate ideas or plans to find creative solutions to difficult problems.

It is important not to allow conflict to become personal. Anna Maravelas (2005) notes that hostility is on the rise as the pressures of modern living create pressure, stress, frustration and anger. The danger is when incivility and rudeness become acceptable norms, which then turn into an escalating pattern. Frustration can be a trigger in which a poorly phrased comment sets off an unintended reaction. She makes the point that statements of contempt have a 'long half life', which can be difficult to smooth over.

There are many different techniques that can be used to resolve interpersonal conflict, but one of my favourites is a tool called Fault Free Conflict Management and the Evil Genius. You can find more details on how the tool works at http://teamcoachingtoolkit.com/fault-free-conflict-management/

Sustain/support

When a crisis hits or when the team is working through a period of intense pressure, leadership must consider which strategies and tactics will best support the sub-teams and help sustain them. The challenge is to try to create an environment where the mood of the team remains positive and optimistic, despite the difficulties they must work through.

Being part of a group stimulates strong emotions, which are sometimes consciously, but more often subconsciously, picked up by others in close proximity. These emotions are strong and primitive. When a group is under pressure, the emotional dynamics will become more intense as each member of the team reacts to the signals coming from the others. This can have both positive and negative consequences. A resilient team will often find their own collective coping mechanisms such as the use of humour to release tension, or the use of analysis and reflection.

Part of the answer lies in maintaining a sense of control. As mentioned above, one of the most common causes of stress is a sense that we have no control over the demands on our resources, and yet we are still held accountable. Complex situations are inevitably going to throw up scenarios that are out of your control. A sense of control comes from being able to distinguish between those issues that you can do something about and those that, for the moment at least, are beyond the influence of the team. It is therefore often a matter of maintaining perspective, and dealing with those tasks that are to hand.

One way to regain a sense of control is to have a plan that has the collective agreement of the team. In a crisis you can only deal with what is in front of you, so the plan can be very short-term focused, and where resources are then allocated to do enough to get through the 'storm'. This short-term goal of survival is often all a team needs to refocus and work together. Other plans and priorities can be set aside to get everyone facing in the same direction.

An important aspect of control is to take responsibility for the situation. A common trap for many teams under pressure is to begin to see themselves as victims, and seek to blame their situation on others such as the project sponsors, stakeholders or other sub-teams. Once a team see themselves as victims, they give up emotional control of the situation. When faced with setbacks, there will inevitably be a desire to find a cause. As the group starts to criticize others for their mishaps, it is important to contain the discussion and pull everyone back to the point that the team must take responsibility whatever is happening inside the project. Resilience comes from accepting the situation, agreeing a plan and then taking action.

Recover

As discussed above, every person has a limit to their ability to remain resilient. The brain is no different to any other part of the body and it needs time to recover from periods of intense activity. The human body repairs itself best when at rest, and so it is essential that time is taken to allow individuals to catch up on sleep and have a period of leisure time when their minds are not required to continually work on mentally and physically demanding tasks.

There is a growing body of evidence indicating that most people can only sustain about 40 hours of high-intensity work over a seven-day period. Beyond that time we start to make mistakes, creating additional work for ourselves and others to correct them. When designing your team's work routines, you should avoid the temptation to assume your team can continually produce high levels of output for more than 40 hours a week. There are likely to be times when the pressure is on and you will need to call on the team to put in additional effort. If your default is to expect your staff to regularly work 50 to 60 hours a week, you have a limited ability to ask for more effort to manage an unexpected crisis.

Despite the growing awareness in many large organizations of the need to encourage employees to maintain aspects of their physical and mental health, firms with an orange-stage mindset still have a tendency to regard people as replaceable resources. This is an antiquated view that ignores the problems that occur when a valued team member leaves the project or, even worse, suffers from burnout. Even if one chooses to ignore the human cost, losing knowledge and experience that can only be developed by working on the project is expensive and time-consuming to replace. Recovery time is essential to sustained performance, and should be planned in advance whenever a team is going through an extended period of pressure.

Reflect

As illustrated in the sailing case story, working through a period of pressure can often be the moment that a group of individuals starts to work together as a real team. To really get the best out of a group of people, it is worth getting into the habit doing a regular debrief after every cycle period of intense activity. Even the most experienced teams can continually learn from each other. We should not, however, take it for granted this learning will happen by simple osmosis.

Adults learn best by talking about their experiences out loud, discussing the events and stories of their peers. However, unless time is formally set aside to review and reflect on recent events, learning opportunities are often lost as everyone moves on to the next challenge. The more frequent the reflection process, the more familiar and comfortable the team is likely to become with this activity. Talking out loud is a great way of helping the mind recover from the difficulties experienced during a period of stress. The process is often cathartic. When team members start to become comfortable talking about their feelings as well as their thoughts, the team really starts to bond. Revealing our feelings can be difficult, but once one person on the team shows they are prepared to admit a degree of vulnerability, the more likely it is that others will also share more personal information. This process can therefore not only speed recovery, but also build the team's collective ability to manage future situations and anticipate what might happen as they move into the next cycle of activity.

Transitions

One of the features often ignored in large projects is the process of transitioning from one major stage to another. The project lifecycle can be seen to move through a series of phases, which starts with studies on feasibility and moves through to final commissioning and handover. The team's resilience strategy should be aware of the potential issues that may arise as one stage comes to an end and another one starts. Whilst programme charts tend to show a definite date that separates the two, the reality is that, from a social perspective, there is a transitioning phase, as people wind down the current stage and prepare for the next.

Transitioning can lead to a drop in performance that can catch the leadership team by surprise if they do not anticipate it. As discussed earlier, teams tend to work to a set of routines, which will inevitably be disrupted by the transition process. At an individual level, change tends to create a level of uncertainty that can reduce motivation. For some, the end of a stage signals the end of their involvement with the project and so part of their concentration is focused on the next project. Behaviours in the teams may change and collaboration diminish if uncertainty increases beyond a critical point.

On a major project, preparing for the new stage whilst completing the final elements of the current stage creates the need for a high level of interaction between different parties, each having to anticipate what will be required, but lacking detailed information. A new phase of work will also bring in new people and new sub-teams, each of which needs to adapt to the new environment. We have discussed the challenges of projects as temporary organizations, but shifts in stages can often require the shift, at least in part, to a new temporary organization. Project leaders should spend time considering the implication of project transitions and the concept of 'liminality' where those involved must learn to occupy a position at, or on both sides of, a boundary or threshold.

It is very easy in a transition period to become absorbed in the technical and commercial aspects of the next stage, but leaders and managers should also be thinking about the social impact. A good question to consider is 'what sort of relationships do we need for this next stage to succeed?' Do not make the mistake of assuming that stable collaborative relationships will easily transfer across. As new people and new sub-teams join, the dynamics within the Big Team will shift, particularly if there has been a change in the commercial arrangements.

Teams may therefore need to be socially recommissioned using the set-up framework explained in Chapter 4, with a repeated emphasis on vision, values, culture and collaborative behavioural norms.

Another element to note is the importance of endings. Too many teams allow themselves to dissolve slowly rather than work to a planned process. Ending any phase of work should involve a process of review and assessment of the team's performance. Managing endings is also important from a social perspective. Teams may end slowly as the workload tapers out and individuals leave to move onto other projects, or may end abruptly due to changes in project strategy or in the external environment. Whatever the pace, humans across the world have worked out the need to mark endings with some form of social celebration, be it a formal meal or a drink at a local pub. Michael West (2012, p. 91) observes that such celebrations and formal leave takings are an important ritual recognizing the significance of the team as a social and task unit and they provide a positive closure to the teams life, enabling members to move on. Such rituals are important in human society and should not be neglected in organizational settings – their symbolic and emotional significance punctuate satisfactorily for its members and the work of the team.

Summary

As with the other models presented throughout the book, the six-step resilience sequence is intended to provide a framework that can be adapted to suit the needs of all or part of a Big Team at a particular stage in the programme. A team's resilience strategy should therefore be a matter for discussion in the early planning stages, rather than reacting to a decline in output. The better a team is prepared, however, the more it will be able to react positively to periods of pressure and prolonged stress without damaging the health of the team members. When used methodically, the process should actually improve team performance.

Chapter 9
A leap of faith

The contents of this book have taken you through a structure for setting up a Big Team to give it the best opportunity to succeed. I have built up the case for each section from a wide range of research into the effectiveness of people working in teams, supplemented by my own observations and experiences. The structure is not a radically new approach, in that all of the ideas, concepts and activities have been used successfully by others. The component parts of leadership, culture, team set-up and team engagement are familiar to anyone who has a frequent involvement in major projects. The framework is nevertheless novel insofar as it places the human components at the centre of project planning, whereas common management practice allows them to drift to the periphery.

I have no doubts that the mechanisms set out in each chapter are effective. In the last seven years, I have seen many examples of a turnaround in the performance of teams that have adopted these practices. I have seen many more projects that have struggled through a lack of understanding of the need to pay attention early in the project cycle to dysfunctional team dynamics.

Having read this far, you now have a framework built around the team performance model that will provide a structure to plan your Big Team strategy. You now know what needs to be done. The next problem is how to deliver it all. On a major project there is a lot to do, and the practical implementation of the various activities is time-consuming, particularly where they require time to be spent on preparation and follow-up.

In the same way that project leaders are not expected to take care of all of the technical or commercial details, you should make provision in your budgets to employ individuals who can run the social cohesion element of the strategy plan. Implementing a programme approach to Big Team set-up requires administrative support as coordination and communication cannot and should not be left to technical engineers and project managers to squeeze around their day jobs. It is far more effective to pay someone, probably with fewer qualifications but more suited to the role, than to use expensive professional time on tasks they do not have the time to tackle with the organizational detail that is required to do them properly.

At a more specialist level, there is a periodic need for support in shaping a team's behaviours or helping teams work out their problems. The use of an experienced project practitioner who can work with a team as its *team coach* can be invaluable in helping improve team effectiveness. Project team coaching is an emerging specialism within the ever-growing coaching profession. The role can be defined as (Llewellyn 2015, p. 20):

> the application of a series of interventions that enable a project team to develop and implement the collaborative behaviours required to deliver the desired outcomes of the stakeholders, to the performance standards that the team expect of themselves.

A team coach is most effective when they are able to position themselves part inside the team and part outside, as illustrated in Figure 9.1. That part of their role that sits inside the team allows them to become familiar with the members of the team, building relationships to the point they are trusted. This trust is important as the role of team coach is often to 'hold up a mirror' to the team to see themselves, so they can make their own corrections.

When inside the team, the coach has a shared commitment to achieving the team's goals and objectives. By remaining on the periphery, however, they are also able to maintain a neutral perspective, and can provide a dispassionate view of the team's formal and informal behaviours. The team coach can work at a number of levels, from the design and facilitation of team set-up activities, through to coaching the senior team to function as an effective unit of leadership. This is perhaps the distinction from an external consultant. A consultant may provide useful observations and make recommendations for improvement. Their advice will nevertheless be ignored or rejected on the basis that 'he/she is not one of us, and does not really understand our issues'.

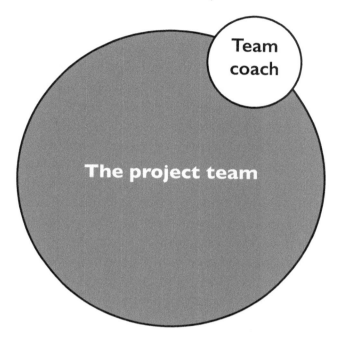

Figure 9.1 The positioning of a project team coach

Despite the advantages a team coach can bring, clients and sponsors often baulk at the suggestion of using another expensive consultant, and there remains a strong resistance to make provision in the budget for the support needed to embed the right behaviours that have been shown to improve team performance. And yet, somehow, money is always found to fix the unexpected problems that indelibly occur downstream. I have found throughout my career that organizations will spend on average five times more to rectify a problem than it would have cost to put some early preventative measures in place!

Finding a budget for building a collaborative team of teams can often be a struggle, particularly when presenting to an organization with a strong orange mindset. I am periodically challenged by the question 'how can you prove this collaborative stuff works?' I can produce numerous examples of very large projects that come in on time and within budget where collaborative teamwork principles were used. I can also point to the research and writing of others who have come to similar conclusions, and yet there often remains an element of doubt unless my evidence has an almost exact correlation with the sponsor's sector. My ultimate counter-question is to ask whether anyone can show me a major project where traditional command-and-control practices have produced a satisfactory result.

In the face of such resistance it is easy to fall back into a familiar, top-down, process-driven approach. Even when your instinct is telling you that it is not going to work effectively. As mentioned above, many of the examples of successful projects that I have encountered have adopted the Big Team framework, but only after realizing that the traditional command-and-control structure was not working. It begs the question as to why we are so slow to adopt new ways of working. There are many reasons and excuses but much of the blame for holding onto ineffective practices lies in the mindset of an older generation who mistrusts change or a young generation who has yet to learn that brute force only produces limited success.

The large complex projects of the 21st century are not, however, sufficiently accommodating to allow such 'old-world' thinking to predominate. I would therefore urge you to be brave and hold to your instincts. If you believe that the concepts in this book will provide a better alternative, then be prepared to push back, and find the time and the budget to set the project up to succeed rather than stumble. Hold on to a framework that enables you to find the right leaders and pull them together into an interconnected network that will form an aligned, engaged and resilient Big Team.

References

Allinger, M. A., Cerasoli, C. P., Tennenbaum, S. I. & Vessey, W. B. (2015) Team resilience: how teams flourish under pressure, *Organizational Dynamics* 44: 176–184.

Alvesson, M. & Spicer, A. (2016) *The Stupidity Paradox, The Power and Pitfalls of Functional Stupidity at Work*, London: Profile Books.

Ancona, D. & Caldwell, D. (1990) Information technology and workgroups: the case new product teams. In J. Galegher, R. Kraut & C. Egido (Eds), *Intellectual Teamwork: Social and Technological Foundations of Cooperative Work* (pp. 173–190), Hillsdale, NJ: Lawrence Erlbaum.

Ansoff, I. O. (1984) *Implanting Strategic Management*, London: Prentice Hall.

Association of Project Management (2018) *Systems Thinking: How Is it Used in Project Management?*, www.apm.org.uk/media/17308/systems-thinking_final.pdf (accessed 12 October 2019).

Bass, B. M. (1990) *Bass & Stogdill's Handbook of Leadership Theory, Research and Managerial Applications*, third edn, New York: Free Press.

Bremer, M. (2018) *Developing a Positive Culture Where People and Performance Thrive*, Melbourne, FL: Motivational Press.

Brown, K., Meyer, N. & Ettenson, R. (2017) Project your project from escalating doubts, *Sloan MIT Management Review*, February 2017.

Bryman, A. (1996) Leadership in organizations. In S. R. Clegg, C. Hardy & W. R. Nord (Eds), *The SAGE Handbook of Organizational Studies* (pp. 276–292), London: Sage.

Cameron, K. S. & Quinn, R. E. (1999) *Diagnosing and Changing Organizational Culture*, Reading, MA: Addison-Wesley.

Cavanagh, M. (2012) *Second Order Project Management*, Farnham: Gower.

Cleden, D. (2009) *Managing Project Uncertainty*, Farnham: Gower.

Clutterbuck, D. (2007) *Coaching the Team at Work*, London: Nicholas Brealey.

Coleman, S. & MacNicol, D. (2015) *Project Leadership*, third edn, Farnham: Gower.

Crevani, L., Lindgren, M. & Packendorff, J. (2007) Shared leadership: a post heroic perspective on leadership as a collective construction, *International Journal of Leadership Studies* 3(1): 40–67.

Duhigg, C. (2016) *Smarter, Faster, Better: The Secrets of Being Productive*, London: Random House.

Edmondson, A. (1999) Psychological safety and learning behaviour in work teams, *Administrative Science Quarterly* 44(2): 350–383.

Forsyth, D. & Kelly, K. (1996) Heuristic based biases in estimates of personal contributions to collective endeavours. In J. Nye & A. Brower (Eds), *What's Social about Social Cognition? Research on Shared Social Cognition in Small Groups* (pp. 106–123), Thousand Oaks, CA: Sage.

Fussell, C. (2017) *One Mission: How Leaders Build a Team of Teams*, London: Macmillan.

Grint, K. (2010) *Leadership: A Very Short Introduction*, Oxford: Oxford University Press.

Gittel, J. H., Cameron, K., Lim, S. & Rivas, V. (2006) Relationship, layoff, and organizational resilience: airline industry responses to September 11, *Journal of Applied Behavioral Science* 42(3): 300–329.

Hawkins, P. (2017) *Leadership Team Coaching: Developing Collective Transformational Leadership*, third edn, London: Kogan Page.

Hersey, P. & Blanchard, K. (1982) *Management of Organizational Behaviour: Utilizing Human Resources*, fourth edn, Englewood Cliffs, NJ: Prentice Hall.

Hofstede, G. (1991) *Cultures and Organizations: Software of the Mind*, first edn, New York: McGraw-Hill.

Katzenbach, J. R. & Smith, D. K. (1993) *The Wisdom of Teams: Creating the High-performance Organization*, Boston, MA: Harvard Business School Press.

Kolb, D. (1984) *Experiential Learning: Experience as the Source of Learning and Development*, Englewood Cliffs, NJ: Prentice-Hall.

Kutsch, E., Hall, M. & Turner, N. (2015) *Project Resilience: The Art of Noticing, Interpreting, Preparing, Containing and Recovering*, Abingdon: Gower.

Laloux, F. (2014) *Reinventing Organizations: A Guide to Creating Organizations Inspired by the Next Stage of Human Consciousness*, Brussels: Nelson Parker.

Lencioni, P. (2005) *Overcoming the Five Dysfunctions of a Team: A Field Guide*, San Francisco, CA: Jossey-Bass.

Levi, D. (2017) *Group Dynamics for Teams*, fifth edn, Thousand Oaks, CA: Sage.

Llewellyn, T. (2015) *Performance Coaching for Complex Projects: Influencing Behaviour and Enabling Change*, Abingdon: Gower.

Llewellyn, T. & Moore, E. (2019) Early warning systems: the missing link. In C. O'Neil (Ed.), *Global Construction Success* (pp. 99–105), Chichester: John Wiley & Sons.

McCann, J. & Selsky, J. W. (2012) *Mastering Turbulence: The Essential Capabilities of Agile and Resilient Individuals, Teams and Organizations*, San Francisco, CA: Jossey-Bass.

McCrystal, S. (2015) *Team of Teams: New Rules of Engagement for a Complex World*, London: Random House.

McGrath, J. (1990) Time matters in groups. In J. Galegher, R. Kraut & C. Egido (Eds), *Intellectual Teamwork: Social and Technological Foundations of Cooperative Work* (pp. 173–190), Hillsdale, NJ: Lawrence Erlbaum.

McIntyre, R. & Salas, E. (1995) Measuring and managing for team performance: lessons from complex environments. In R. Guzzo & E. Sals (Eds), *Team Effectiveness and Decision-making in Organizations* (pp. 9–45), San Francisco, CA: Jossey-Bass.

Maravelas, A. (2005) *How to Reduce Workplace Conflict and Stress*, Franklin Lakes, NJ: Career Press.

Meadows, D. H. (2008) *Thinking in Systems: A Primer*, White River Junction, VT: Chelsea Green Publishing.

Meneghel, I., Martinez, I. M. & Salanova, M. (2016) Job-related antecedents of team resilience and improved team performance, *Personnel Review* 45(3): 505–522.

Merrow, E. W. & Nandurdikar, N. (2018) *Leading Complex Projects: A Data-driven Approach to Mastering the Human Side of Project Management*, Hoboken, NJ: John Wiley and Sons.

Nikander, I. O. (2010) Early warnings: a phenomenon in project management, doctoral dissertation (unpublished). Cited in T. Williams, O. J. Klakegg, D. H. T. Walker, B. Andersen & O. M. Magnussen (2012) Identifying and acting on early warning signals in complex projects, *Project Management Journal* April: 37–53.

Pearce, C. L. & Conger, J. A. (2003) *Shared Leadership: Reframing the Hows and Whys of Leadership*, London: Sage.

Pink, D. (2009) *Drive: The Surprising Truth about What Motivates Us*, New York: Penguin.

Radecki, D. & Hull, L. (2018) *Psychological Safety: The Key to Happy High Performing People and Teams*, n.p.: Academy of Brain-based Leadership.

Rameezdeen, R. & Gunarathna, N. (2003) Disputes and construction industry cultures, *AACE International Transactions* 24: 1–8.

Riolli, L. & Savicki, V. (2003) Information system organizational resilience, *Omega* 31(3): 227–233.

Robertson, P. (2005) *Always Change a Winning Team: Why Reinvention and Change are Pre-requisites for Business Success*, Singapore: Marshall Cavendish.

Schein, E. H. & Schein, P. A. (2018) *Humble Leadership: The Power of Relationships, Openness and Trust*, Oakland, CA: Berrett-Koelher.

Senge, P. (1990) *The Fifth Discipline: The Art and Practice of the Learning Organization*, New York: Doubleday.

Sherif, M. (1966) *In Common Predicament: Social Psychology of Intergroup Conflict and Cooperation*, Boston, MA: Houghton Mifflin.

Sneddon, J. (2003) *Freedom from Command and Control: A Better Way to Make Work Work*, Buckingham: Vanguard Education.

Stacey, R. D. (2003) *Strategic Management and Organisational Dynamics: The Challenge of Complexity*, fourth edn, London: Prentice Hall.

Suroweicki, J. (2005) *The Wisdom of Crowds: Why the Many Are Smarter than the Few*, New York: First Anchor Books.

Tajfel, H. & Turner, J. (1986) The social identity theory of intergroup behaviour. In S. Worchel & W. Austin (Eds), *Psychology of Intergroup Relations* (pp. 2–24), Chicago, IL: Nelson Hall.

Taylor, F. W. (1911) *The Principles of Scientific Management*, New York: Harper & Brothers.

Tuckman, W. T. & Jensen, M. C. (1977) Stages of small group development revisited, *Group & Organization Studies* 2(4): 419–427.

Tyssen, A. K., Wald, A. & Speith, P. (2013) The challenge of transactional and transformational leadership in projects, *International Journal of Project Management* 32: 365–375.

Watkins, M. (2012) How managers become leaders, *Harvard Business Review*, June.

Weisinger, H. & Pawliw-Fry, J. P. (2015) *How to Perform under Pressure: The Science of Doing Your Best When it Matters Most*, London: John Murray Learning.

West, M. A. (2012) *Effective Teamwork: Practical Lessons from Organizational Research*, Chichester: John Wiley and Sons.

Williams, T., Klakegg, O. J., Walker, D. H. T., Andersen, B. & Magnussen, O. M. (2012) Identifying and acting on early warning signals in complex projects, *Project Management Journal* April: 37–53.

Index